Collins

Autumn: oil on canvas (1573) by Giuseppe Arcimboldo

Mushroom Miscellany

PATRICK HARDING

Collins

I dedicate this book to Chloe, my ancient Jack Russell. Much of the book was planned during our daily walks together. I am also indebted to my nieces Charlotte and Sarah for their valuable comments and corrections at the manuscript stage. Finally thanks to my wife Jean and daughter Bryony for putting up with me while I was writing the book and good luck to my son Martin who sensibly moved out before I started.

This edition produced for The Book People Ltd, Parc Menai, Bangor LL57 4FB

First published in 2008 by Collins
an imprint of HarperCollins*Publishers*
77–85 Fulham Palace Road
London W6 8JB
www.collins.co.uk

A catalogue record for this book is available from the British Library
ISBN-13 978 0 00 782892 0

Publisher: Myles Archibald
Editor: Charlotte Pover
Designed by Richard Marston
Production: Keeley Everitt
Printed and bound in China by RR Donnelley
09 08
5 4 3 2 1

Contents

Boletus edulis (early 19th century) by Paul Louis Oudart

No Ceps Please, We're British

In the autumn of 1981 I taught my first residential weekend course on Mushrooms and Toadstools. On the Friday evening the small group of participants joined me for a preprandial drink. It was not long before I discovered that each of them had a similar tale to tell. The stories all included accounts of the jaw-dropping response of family and colleagues when told of the reason for their weekend away. In those days very few shops stocked anything other than white cultivated mushrooms which were usually neatly displayed in blue cardboard punnets. Field and other 'wild' mushrooms were largely left alone.

As for those people who collected and ate 'toadstools', they were considered to be either wildly eccentric or of European extraction. I was placed in the former category when, in 1983, *The Guardian* Diary section included a preview of seasonal entertainments offered by the Youth Hostel Association:

> *Curiosities like a voodoo evening at Boggle Hole in Robin Hood's Bay are available, or an Esperanto weekend in the Peak District. First prize for an offbeat break, though, must go to the 'fungus foray' based at Edale on the weekend of October 7th–9th. For an extra £6 you can join mycologist Dr Patrick Harding collecting blewits, chanterelles and boletus [sic] edulis and consuming them in a 'fungus feast'.*

Five years later I was invited to teach a mushroom course on behalf of Cambridge University's Adult Education Department, based at Madingley Hall. The silver service dinner on the Friday was preceded by a resonant gong and full Latin grace. Prior to the coffee, the warden addressed the assembled company:

> *Welcome to Madingley and to a fascinating range of weekend courses. 'Unexplored Mozart' will take place in the Saloon; those 'Reading Greek' will be in the Library while 'Mushrooms and Toadstools' will be …*

Her voice was drowned by the rising tide of laughter from the musicians and linguists as I tried to appear invisible. By the Saturday evening I had recovered my composure and made my own announcement before the coffee was served:

Those of you studying Mozart and Greek are more than welcome to pay a brief visit to the board room, where you might be interested to see what those on the Mushroom course have been up to.

Spread across eight tables were scores of labelled specimens collected on our field trip. Two years later, when the course was repeated, I was delighted to welcome among the course members two from the Greek and three from the Mozart group. Twenty years on and the mushroom course is still running. It is heavily oversubscribed.

Mushroom hunters of European extraction included Polish immigrants who had settled in Britain during and immediately after World War II. Collecting and eating fungi is an important part of Polish culture and those in the vanguard of the more recent influx must have been pleasantly surprised by the lack of local competition when it came to mushroom hunting. A Polish dish traditionally served on Christmas Eve includes *Boletus edulis* in the list of ingredients.

Old English books about cookery and mushrooms mentioned *Boletus edulis* under its local name of penny bun. This moniker arose on account of the likeness of the pale-brown, slightly sticky, convex cap to a product displayed in many bakers and which had originally sold for just one (old) penny. In the years following World War II the bakers' penny bun lost its fight against inflation while the mushroom lost the battle to keep its old English name. As British cooks looked for inspiration from French cuisine so the writers of cookery books anglicised the French name for the fungus *Cèpe* and penny bun became known as cep.

British cooks have rarely suffered from a shortage of recipe books; if anything the problem has been more one of surfeit rather than deficiency. The same cannot be said of books about mushrooms and toadstools; although like buses, after a long wait, several turned up at once. Lack of interest in edible mushrooms has long bordered on a phobia in Britain; a condition not helped by a paucity of non-technical books aimed at the general public.

Mordecai Cooke did his best in Victorian times with publications such as *British Edible Fungi – How to Distinguish and to Cook Them*. The British Government's attempts to encourage fungal foraging, especially during times of food shortage, resulted in *Edible and Poisonous Fungi* – Bulletin No 23 of the Ministry of Agriculture and Fisheries, first published in 1910. This slim booklet described just 19 edible 'varieties' and nine poisonous ones. The remaining stock of the 1945 edition was destroyed by a German incendiary bomb, which may have been a blessing in disguise given that one of the species included in the edible section has since proved to be poisonous, albeit it to a minority of the population.

In the 1960s Findlay's *Wayside and Woodland Fungi* included some illustrations by Beatrix Potter (see page 187), but the book was not aimed at those with a culinary interest in the subject. Richard Mabey's ground-breaking *Food for Free*, first published in 1972, included a section on edible fungi. Three years later Jane Grigson produced her culinary classic, *The Mushroom Feast*, although with only limited mycological information and rather small line drawings. In the same year Shirley Conran included the following advice in Superwoman:

> *I'd rather lie on a sofa than sweep beneath it.*
> *Life is too short to stuff a mushroom.*

At the time the only widely available picture book aimed at the interested amateur, with the exception of The Observer's book, was Lange and Hora's *Collins Guide to Mushrooms and Toadstools*. As a young naturalist I 'bagged' my first 100 species with the help of Lange and Hora, but the quality of the pictures left much to be desired and no English names were included.

In 1981 Roger Phillips paved the way for the interested amateur mycologist with a user-friendly book (recently updated) adorned with excellent photographs and lightened by the inclusion of some English names. By 1986 Britain was almost ready for *How to Identify Edible Mushrooms*, which I wrote with my great friend Tony Lyon. The book is still in print and has been joined by a plethora of others (including *Need to Know? Mushroom Hunting*, published in 2006) on the subject of edible fungi.

For many years local natural history societies paid lip service to fungi with just a single annual foray, but following the upsurge of interest in mycology many groups now have a separate fungal section. In addition, since the 1990s many local fungal recording groups have been formed (see page 204 for details) while journals such as *Field Mycology* and *British Wildlife* keep mycologists up to date with new developments. An interest in fungi is no longer considered unusual; penny buns have become accepted.

Mushrooms or Toadstools?

The *Grete Herbal*, written in 1526, had this to say about what it called 'mussherons':

> *There be two manners of them, one manner is deedly and sleath them that eateth of them and be called tode stoles.*

Given that the other 'manners' were the edible ones, it is interesting to note that this indicates that the group of organisms termed mussherons (mushrooms) *included* the poisonous tode stoles (toadstools). Over the following 400 years the word mushroom came to be restricted to edible species, separate from the inedible toadstools, although it was realised that not all of the latter were poisonous. The title of Edward Step's early 20th century book *Toadstools and Mushrooms of the Countryside* is indicative of the use of the two terms at a time when the common names of edible, if unrelated, species included field mushroom, parasol mushroom and oyster mushroom.

The meaning of the two terms continued in this way until the end of the 20th century, as evident in *Gem Mushrooms and Toadstools* (1996). As the British public became more interested in fungi and in gathering edible ones, so a subtle change occurred. The second edition of the Gem book appeared under the simpler title of *Mushrooms*, as did an updated version of a book by Roger Phillips previously entitled *Mushrooms and Other Fungi of Great Britain and Europe*. After almost 500 years the word mushroom has once again become an all-embracing term for the macrofungi (those that produce fruitbodies that can easily be seen with the naked eye); a group that includes the toadstools.

Scientists also lumped mushrooms and toadstools together, in a group known as the *Agaricales*. The 'agarics', as they became known, include all species with a fleshy, umbrella-shaped fruitbody as typified by fly agaric (*Amanita muscaria*), the infamous red and white toadstool. As knowledge of fungi developed, the agarics were separated into a large number of different genera, each containing closely related species. Professional mycologists reserve the word mushroom for members of the genus *Agaricus*, which have free gills (not attached to the stem), a ring on the stem and dark-brown spores shed from pink gills. The genus includes cultivated mushroom (*Agaricus bisporus*),

FACING PAGE: The Vegetable Market: detail from 15th Century Italian fresco

field mushroom (*Agaricus campestris*) and yellow-staining mushroom (*Agaricus xanthodermus*). Unfortunately, not all members of the genus are safe to eat; *Agaricus xanthodermus* is mildly poisonous. One result of this is the enigma of a poisonous 'mushroom', one reason why the recent list of recommended English names (see page 41) drops the mushroom name in favour of yellow stainer.

If the terms mushroom and toadstool are confusingly interchangeable, the presumed etymology of the two words is equally complex. Several 19th century authors assumed that the word mushroom evolved from mussheron, which came from a French word, *mouscheron*. This was believed to be a derivation of *mouche-eron*, from an old French name for fly agaric (*Amanita muscaria*), which is most people's idea of a toadstool rather than a mushroom. Other writers have attempted to make a link with the French word *mousseron*, still used in reference to certain edible fungi, and the word *mousse*, meaning moss; a habitat often frequented by edible fungi. *Mousse* also means foam or froth (hence the dessert of the same name) and this ties in with the early belief (recorded by Pliny) that fungi developed from a 'kind of glutinous fome or froth'. Sponges were thought to originate in a similar way and this association may be at the root of the word 'fungus', coming from the Greek *sphonggis*, a sponge.

Mushrooms were long believed to be formed from mud or the slime left by snails. This has raised the possibility that the term mushroom originated from the Greek word μυκηζ, giving us the Latin *mucus*, the likely origin of the term mycology, the scientific study of fungi. The word mycology was first used by the Reverend Berkeley in 1836, but it was some time before it replaced the earlier term fungology.

In 1953 John Ramsbottom dared to argue that the derivation of the word toadstool was self-evident:

> *A typical toadstool obviously might serve as a resting place for a sedentary bachtrian.*

His words were backed by a sequence of black and white photographs from *The Times*. These appeared to show a toad climbing on to a toadstool, although the images were later found to have been faked.

While it is unlikely that the average toad spends much of its time sitting on a toadstool (but see page 146) there is a long history associating toads (and frogs) with fungi. The link is also found in names used throughout Europe and also in Africa, America and Japan. The earliest British reference is the word *tadstole* (1398), followed by *toodys hatte* in the 15th century. The link is also clear in the use of the old word paddock, meaning a frog or toad, in the term *paddockstool*. That it was toads rather than frogs that lent their name is probably due to the venomous nature of the former. Like fungi, frogs and toads were associated with mud and slime, but frogs lacked the venomous nature attributed to toads and many species of fungi.

The most poisonous European fungi are found in the genus *Amanita* (see page 129). Here the fruitbody emerges through a sheet-like veil, the remains of which may be left as raised, wart-like spots on the surface of the cap. Some authors have argued that *Amanita muscaria* (fly agaric) is the archetypal toadstool. An earlier English name for it was wart caps; another possible link with the warty-backed toad. In 1953 a related species, *Amanita citrina* (false deathcap), was shown to contain bufotenine, a chemical first isolated from the toxic skin gland secretions of toads. Sadly for those seeking a common link behind the use of both toads and fly agarics for their hallucinogenic effects (see page 151), bufotenine does not occur in fly agaric. In addition, although bufotenine is structurally similar to psilocybin (see page 144), it is not the chemical responsible for the effects of toad's skin gland secretions.

Fungi are often associated with, or look like, animal dung. Tad was an old word for dung. Here is perhaps another derivation for tadstole or tad stool, with the word stool being used with reference to faeces rather than a seat. Some seek to explain a link with both the toad and dung theories via the French word for a toad, *crapaud*, but I consider that this falls between two stools! Finally, *tode* is a German word for death; throwing a different slant on the origin of the word toadstool. I prefer the association with toads, but the true origin of the word toadstool, as with that for mushroom, is lost in the mists of time.

1
2
3
6
5
4
7
8
9
10
11
15
16
14
12
13
21
22

The Fifth Kingdom

The absence of eggs or seeds in the fungi resulted in a long-held belief that they arose by spontaneous generation. During the 17th century the respected naturalist Gaspard Bauchin considered fungi to be 'nothing but the superfluous humidity of soil, trees, rotten wood and other decaying substances'. As late as 1804 it was argued that fungi resulted from shooting stars, even though 75 years earlier Micheli had shown that, under suitable conditions, fungal spores gave rise to the same kind of fungus from which they had originated.

Carl Linnaeus summed up the method of separating the three kingdoms of nature when he wrote in 1751:

> LAPIDES crescunt. VEGETABILIA crescunt & vivunt. ANIMALIA crescunt, vivunt & sentiunt.

This can be translated as 'If a thing simply existed it was mineral. If it lived it was vegetable. If it also had senses then it was an animal'.

Other schemes separated the vegetables (plants) from the animals on the basis of mobility, although this resulted in some scientists placing fungi and sponges in the same group; a problem alluded to by the great Victorian mycologists Cooke (see page 182) and Berkeley who began their book *Fungi Their Nature, Influences and Uses* (1875) with:

> *The most casual observer of Nature recognizes in almost every instance that comes under his notice in every-day life, without the aid of logical definition, the broad distinctions between an animal, a plant, and a stone. To him the old definition that an animal is possessed of life and locomotion, a plant of life without locomotion, and a mineral deficient in both, seems to be sufficient, until some day he travels beyond the circuit of diurnal routine, and encounters a sponge ...*

As long ago as 1784 a Frenchman by the name of Villemet had proposed that there should be three kingdoms: plant, animal and fungal, but for the following 200 years fungi were regarded by both the scientific community and the general public as

FACING PAGE:
Plants and Fungi under the Microscope (late 19th century)

occupying part of the plant kingdom. Professional mycologists worked within university botany departments or in the confines of botanical gardens such as at Kew.

As a child in the 1950s I purchased *The Observer's Book of Common Fungi* and was informed:

> *Fungi belong to the vegetable kingdom but differ fundamentally from all other plants (except for a few degenerate forms) in that they possess no chlorophyll.*

In the 1960s radical new schemes for the classification of living organisms were proposed, but it was not until the 1980s that the concept of grouping living organisms into not two, but five kingdoms became widely accepted. Since then scientists have embraced the notion that fungi belong to the fifth kingdom, separate from animals, plants, Protozoa and Chromista (including bacteria). A quarter of a century on from this reclassification and the majority of the British public, along with sections of the media, have not yet caught up. As late as 2005 a 'plant-tastic' display at the Ashmolean Museum in Oxford depicted a collection of fly agaric toadstools under the title 'Danger! Poisonous Plants'.

One way of looking at the differences between plants, animals and fungi is to sum up their different lifestyles: plants are producers; they manufacture food by the process of photosynthesis with the help of the green pigment chlorophyll and energy from sunlight; animals are consumers that ingest their food; fungi cannot manufacture food, but instead absorb material that they break down externally, they are recyclers.

Plants and fungi can also be separated by morphological and chemical differences. Most plants are made up of cells and cellulose is a principal component of their cell walls. In contrast, most fungi (and all mushrooms and toadstools) are made up of elongated cell-like filaments, the structural component of which is largely chitin, a chemical also found in the wing cases of insects. Some fungi such as the yeasts are single celled but, in common with the filamentous fungi, they lack cellulose.

Plants, fungi and animals are termed eukaryotes: their DNA is packaged in chromosomes within nuclei. Bacteria are more primitive and lack internal structures associated with their genetic blueprint and are known as prokaryotes. It is only recently that some fungal-like organisms, the actinomycetes, have been found to be prokaryotic and are now classed along with bacteria. The strange slime moulds, which have fungal-like methods of reproduction, ingest their food in a manner similar to amoebae and have now been placed with the protozoans. Much more recently, the structure of important membranes (cristae) within the mitochondria ('power stations') of eukaryotes has been shown to be tubular in animals and plants, but flattened in fungi.

In the 19th century, Cooke concluded:

> *It is exceedingly difficult to give a logical definition of what constitutes a fungus.*

Spooner and Roberts, writing in 2005, were prepared to give it a try:

> *The Fungi comprise non-photosynthetic eukaryotes with an absorptive nutrition that do not have an amoeboid pseudopodial stage, and may occur as both single celled and multicelled organisms. The cell walls contain chitin and B-glucans, and their mitochondria have flattened cristae.*

A rather more user-friendly definition is:

> *A very diverse assemblage of organisms and micro-organisms that obtain their nutrients from decaying organic material or from living plants, animals or even other fungi.*

Other organisms that have long proved difficult to classify include the lichens, which were frequently grouped with the mosses. It is now known that a lichen consists of two organisms, a fungus and an algal component (or more rarely a type of bacterium). As the algae in lichens are capable of photosynthesis, lichens are more plant-like. As each species of lichen involves a different species of fungus, lichens are now classified by their fungal component and are included within the fifth kingdom of the fungi. Not withstanding this, the lichens differ from other fungi in many ways and have not been included in this book.

How Many Are There?

People often express surprise that fungi have been placed in their own kingdom. This is usually because of an assumption that there are not very many different species of mushroom and toadstool, compared with the number of flowering plants.

Looking at the numbers from a British perspective, there are about 2,000 species of flowering plant growing in the wild. The recently published (2005) *Checklist of the British & Irish Basidiomycota* lists some 2,200 species of mushrooms and toadstools (agarics). In addition, the list includes 430 brackets and relatives, over 100 puffballs and relatives, around 100 club and coral fungi, about 20 hedgehog fungi and over 200 jelly fungi. All of the latter groups are included in books about 'mushrooms' together with some of the larger species of ascomycete (see page 26) such as the morels and truffles, taking the total number to well over 3,000 species of larger fungi. When all the lichens and smaller species of ascomycete are included along with the moulds and yeasts, together with plant parasites known as rusts and smuts we reach a figure in excess of 14,000 named species of fungi in Britain.

With the exception of garden escapees and deliberately introduced plants there have been very few newly discovered British species of flowering plant during the past 20 years. In contrast, species of larger fungi that have not previously been recorded in Britain are being discovered every year. Some of these may well be new to Britain (see page 29), but others represent native species that have previously escaped the attention of anyone capable of identifying them. As the number of both amateur and professional mycologists has grown so has our knowledge of the diversity of different fungal species in Britain.

Esher Common in Surrey, a 380 hectare site within easy reach of London (and the mushroom experts at Kew) has probably undergone more mycological recording than anywhere else in Britain, which means that it is possibly the best recorded area anywhere in the world. To date, over 3,200 species of fungi have been found there and new ones are being added to the list every year. The fact that there has been at least one professional mycologist based at Kew Gardens for the past 125 years, in conjunction with over a

FACING PAGE:
Fairy Inkcap – *Coprinus disseminatus*

century of recording by members of the British Mycological Society, has left Britain with a wealth of fungal records.

Despite this, knowledge concerning the distribution of larger fungi in Britain is very patchy and some parts of the country are under-recorded; areas with many records may reflect the close proximity of a good mycologist rather than a region that is especially rich in fungi. Although some new records of the larger fungi reflect habitat and climate change (see pages 59 and 33), others are the result of keen observation and perseverance in attempts to identify species that are not featured in books about British fungi. That this can involve amateur mushroom hunters is explained in Chapter Six.

While new records of larger fungi are still relatively uncommon, the number of newly discovered species of microfungi is much higher. In many cases these prove to be not just new records for Britain, but species that are new to science. One example is a fungus that grows on the fallen leaves of woody plants with leathery leaves, including the strawberry tree (*Arbutus unedo*). During the time that I was writing this book I heard a programme on Radio 4 about this newly discovered species. It has very unusual spore-bearing structures, unlike any previously described. My study window overlooks the front garden, which is home to a 10-year-old strawberry tree. I am looking forward to making a close (microscopic) examination of the decaying leaves from under the plant; there is always something new to look out for in the fungus world.

One of the principal aims of naturalists has been the classification and accurate naming of species; only when this is done can we answer the question, 'How many species are there?' The Swedish naturalist Carl Linnaeus may have revolutionised the classification and naming of plants in the middle of the 18th century, but he never came to terms with the fungi. In 1751 he wrote:

> *The order of Fungi, a scandal to art, is still chaos with botanists not knowing what a species, what a variety.*

In one of his publications he included the fungi under the name Chaos, and even in his magnum opus of plant classification (*Species Plantarum*) published in 1753, he included only 10 genera of fungi and a total of just 90 species, despite the earlier work of an Italian mycologist who had listed over 900 species. It was left to Christiaan Persoon to sort out the chaos of the fungi. The man who was to do for fungi what Linnaeus did for flowering plants was born in the Cape of Good Hope in the early 1760s, was sent as a teenager to school in Germany and finally settled in Paris. His publications included books on the lower plants and four important works on the classification of fungi. His system of fungal classification was largely based on the morphology of the fruiting bodies and most of the 100 genera that he created are still recognised today.

The next great taxonomic mycologist was born in the last decade of the 18th century and had a background that was remarkably similar to that of Linnaeus, who was born nearly 90 years earlier. Like Linnaeus, Elias Fries was born in southern Sweden and was the son of a clergyman. Both men went to the same school and ultimately both became Professor of Botany at the University of Uppsala. Fries recorded the event that was to start his interest in fungi. As a 12-year-old he was picking wild strawberries when he found a large specimen of a species of *Hericium*, a beautiful creamy-white fungus that looks like a cross between a coral and a mass of stalactites.

As with the method Linnaeus used to classify plants, many of the fungal classification schemes devised by Fries are now little used, but his knowledge of fungi enabled him to describe, name and study nearly 5,000 species, including many from outside his native country. Fries concentrated on the agarics (mushrooms and toadstools), where he was the first person to use spore colour to separate different groups, a feature still considered important by modern taxonomists. Fries died in 1878 and so was a contemporary of two of Britain's great 19th century mycologists, the Reverend Berkeley and Mordecai Cooke (see page 182).

Because there was a long-held belief that fungi were the result of the devil's work, the study of fungi was not approved by the Church until the 19th century, by which time knowledge about mammals, birds and flowering plants was already at an advanced stage. Watling has commented that as a result of this the scientific understanding of fungi lags 100 years behind that of many organisms.

The 20th century continued to produce eminent European and North American mycologists. Of the latter, one character was Curtis Lloyd who, before he died in 1926, became one of the leading experts in puffballs and their relatives. He once bought the stock of a failed shoe shop for the sake of the boxes to house his collection. He was not above playing a joke on his fellow mycologists and even named a fictitious puffball *Lycoperdon anthropomorphus*.

The work of European and American mycologists has resulted in a fairly good knowledge of at least the larger fungi in many northern temperate parts of the world.

Good and Bad Mushrooms (*c.* 1900)

Despite this there is a paucity of information about fungi in tropical and subtropical regions, where the diversity of plant and animal species is at its greatest. It is for this reason that estimates of the total number of fungal species in the world remain guesswork. Writing in 1981, Rod Cooke introduced his book *Fungi* with:

> *There are over* 50,000 *known kinds of fungi, and it has been estimated that about* 200,000 *more await discovery.*

A quarter of a century later the number of known, named species is in the region of 100,000, and the total has been estimated to be closer to 1.5 million different species. The figure of 1.5 million has been arrived at by observations, spanning a range of habitats, that the number of fungal species is, on average, six times greater than the number of flowering plant species. This ratio also works for Britain as a whole, as there are approximately 12,000 named species of fungus and some 2,000 species of flowering plant.

Some scientists believe that the global figure for the number of fungal species may be much higher, particularly as many insects, mosses and ferns appear to harbour unique, but largely unstudied, species of fungus. One estimate has put the worldwide fungal species count as closer to 9 million. Whatever the true figure there is plenty of work to be done: every year mycologists at Kew name about 1,500 new species, collected from all over the world. That we may have named as few as 1% of the world's fungal species is indicative of just how little we know.

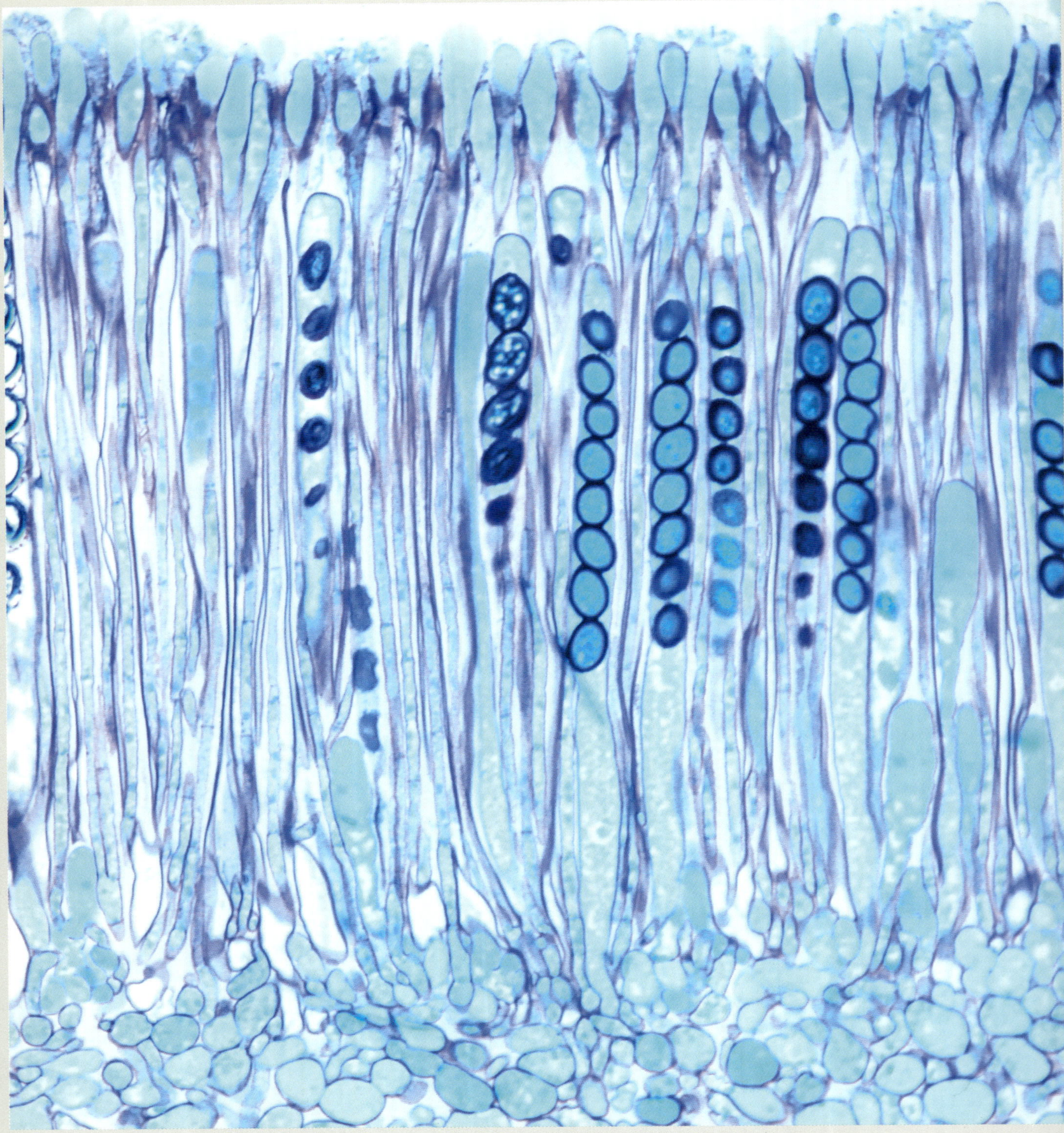

Fungi, Folders and Files

The information stored in a computer needs to be readily accessible. To ensure this, individual inputs are given file names and grouped with other similar files in a named folder. Folders are themselves grouped under named categories, one example being the different users of the computer. This hierarchical pigeonholing of data into discrete bundles is analogous to the methods of classification into groups (taxa) used by taxonomists seeking to categorise species of living organism. Just as different computer users have different systems of grouping their stored information, so taxonomists differ in the way that they classify organisms. It is only since the latter part of the 20th century that the fungi, the group that include mushrooms, have been placed in their own discrete folder, often referred to as the fifth kingdom (see Chapter Three).

The problem for mycologists is how best to place the world's 100,000 named species (equivalent to 100,000 files) into groups (folders, etc.) that reflect the similarity and evolutionary relationship of the species within each group. Given that the scientific names (and as a result the common names; see Chapter Eight) of species reflect the groups into which they are placed, the classification system has important knock-on effects.

Until relatively recently all major groups of the fungal kingdom were separated by features such as the shape of the fruitbody and colour of the spores, or by details visible with an ordinary microscope. The latter includes the nature of the spore-producing tissue, the size, shape and ornamentation of the spores and details of the hyphal threads. Such classification systems invariably resulted in assemblages of fungi that had only one thing in common: they did not fit anywhere else. Most systems were far from perfect. The use of the electron microscope, chemical analysis and, above all, genetic analysis including the sequencing of DNA has resulted in a major regrouping of many fungal species. One result of this reclassification has been a change to the scientific names of some fungi, including species of mushroom and toadstool. In addition, some species formerly included within the fungal kingdom have been moved to other kingdoms.

Most mycologists now recognise five main groups (phyla) within the fungal

FACING PAGE:
Section of an Ascomycete Fungus showing ascospores

kingdom. These are Basidiomycota, Ascomycota, Glomeromycota, Zygomycota and Chytdridiomycota.

Members of the Basidiomycota produce sexual spores *on the surface* of special club-shaped cells known as basidia. The agarics, a historical term for mushrooms and toadstools with a mushroom-shaped fruitbody, belong in the Basidiomycota, in a class known as the basidiomycetes. Older schemes divided the agarics into some five orders, largely based on spore colour. Current thinking is to have just three orders: one order includes the boletes, such as the edible cep (*Boletus edulis*), with tubes in place of gills; a second embraces the crumblecaps (*Russula* spp.) and milkcaps (*Lactarius* spp.), typical of woodland habitats; and a third includes all other agarics.

The basidiomycetes also include puffballs and their relatives, bracket and crust-forming fungi, club and coral fungi, and most of the larger jelly fungi. Two other classes of Basidiomycota include the rusts, smuts and other plant parasites; in total, around 500 British species of microfungi which, unlike the basidiomycetes, do not produce large fruitbodies.

Candlesnuff fungus – *Xylaria hypoxylon*

Members of the Ascomycota, usually referred to as the ascomycetes, produce sexual spores *inside* elongated sac-shaped cells known as asci. This group includes morels and truffles which, along with some cup-fungi such as orange-peel fungus (*Aleuria aurantia*), have relatively large fruitbodies and are usually included in books about mushrooms. The ascomycetes also embrace thousands of species of cup fungi with miniature fruitbodies only a few millimetre across, most of which grow on rotting plant material. Those in a group known as the flask fungi also have tiny fruitbodies, but in a few species these are clumped together in a larger mass of black tissue; examples include King Alfred's cakes (*Daldinia concentrica*) and the aptly-named candlesnuff fungus (*Xylaria hypoxylon*). Another very large group of ascomycete fungi have entered into symbiotic relationships with primitive algae or bacteria in organisms known as lichens.

Other ascomycotous microfungi include species that cause plant galls, such as witches' broom on birch and leaf curl on peach. The group includes the commercially important singled-celled fungi known as yeasts. These frequent sugar-rich habitats such as ripe fruit and are essential aids for the making of leavened bread and alcohol. Powdery mildews on plants and a range of moulds are also included here. Many of these rarely, if ever, produce sexual spores, but spread by asexual means. Among the moulds, many of which contaminate foodstuffs including bread and jam, is one called *Penicillium chrysogenum*, the original species from which penicillin was isolated (see page 178). In Britain there are at least 5,500 named ascomycetes, including over 1,800 cup fungi and about the same number of lichenised species.

The other three phyla of the kingdom Fungi may be of little interest to the average mushroom hunter, but include some very important fungi. Although there are fewer than 20 named British species in the phylum Glomeromycota, they include those that are probably some of the most ubiquitous of all fungi, forming mycorrhizal (fungus root) relationships with a huge range of non-woody plants. Their significance is discussed on page 55. Included in the Zygomycota are common moulds such as species of *Mucor* and fungi that parasitise insects. One of these kills house flies and leaves the moribund insects stuck to window panes, each surrounded by a halo of spores. The final group, Chytridiomycota, has spores that are mobile in liquid. Not surprisingly, many are aquatic or live in damp soil.

Several other groups that were previously considered to be fungi have recently been placed in the kingdom Chromista, although their classification remains a contentious issue. Species in the kingdom Chromista are largely aquatic or require damp conditions. They include the diatoms and some species of seaweed. The most fungal-like organisms now placed with the Chromista include species of *Pythium* which cause 'damping off' among overcrowded seedlings. Species of *Phytophthora*, one of which causes potato blight, have been moved into the kingdom Chromista.

The slime moulds or Myxomycota have also been ejected from the fungal kingdom and now reside in the kingdom Protozoa. Although bearing fungal-like fruitbodies, these organisms are not composed of thread-like hyphae and include a mobile, amoeboid stage as part of their life cycle. In a number of common species this stage is readily visible as sick-like patches of white or yellow, on grass or rotting wood, usually after periods of heavy rainfall.

The Shock of the New

The mentality of the twitcher is not restricted to ornithologists. In 1979 the novelist John Fowles wrote of his experiences in France:

> *I came on my first Military Orchid, a species I had long wanted to encounter, but hitherto never seen outside a book. I fell on my knees before it in a way that all botanists will know. I identified, to be quite certain, with Professors Clapham, Tutin and Warburg in hand (the standard British Flora), I measured, I photographed, I worked out where I was on the map, for future reference. I was excited, very happy, one always remembers one's 'firsts' of the rarer species.*

For mushroom hunters and even professional mycologists, life is not as simple as it is for botanists or ornithologists. First, there are far more species to contend with and many of these can only be identified accurately with the aid of a microscope. Secondly, there is no equivalent book to the British flora or handbook of British birds which describes *all* of the larger fungi that have been recorded from our islands.

For most amateur mycologists the thrill of a new discovery is restricted to identifying a mushroom that is new to the finder rather than new to Britain. Despite this, Carol Hobart, a dedicated amateur mycologist from my home city of Sheffield, has recently discovered two species that are new to Britain. Far from being insignificant little fungi they are both quite large agarics; one a relative of death cap in the genus *Amanita*, the other related to the field mushroom.

There are plenty of fungal species that have not previously been identified in Britain, or anywhere else for that matter; the problem is spotting that they are new and then getting the record verified. Even a record that is new to a region, even if not new to Britain, is important in helping to build a picture of the geographic distribution of the fungus, especially where the species is declining as a result of habitat loss, or spreading, possibly from a single, recent introduction. Just as blurred photographs of 'a bird never seen before in Britain' are unacceptable to the scientific community, the validation of a new fungal record requires back-up material as proof.

FACING PAGE:
Devil's fingers – *Clathrus archeri*, an Australian species now turning up in southern England

The accurate identification of a fungus can rarely be done in the field. At the very least it will require the collection of specimens for further examination later or, if all else fails, to send to an expert. If possible, collect several specimens in all stages of development. Even if the mushroom subsequently turns out to be rare, there is no evidence that collecting fruitbodies will do any more damage than the picking of apples from a fruit tree. Collect the whole fruitbody; do not snap or cut off the stem base as this can result in diagnostic features being left behind. For species growing on wood, try to remove the fruitbody with some of the attached wood. A penknife is an essential part of the mushroom hunter's kit.

Make a record of any features that may disappear in transit. These may include a distinctive smell, texture or colour change brought about by handling the fungus. Mushrooms need to be transported back to base in a manner that prevents them from drying out or being damaged, but never in a plastic bag where they will quickly disintegrate into a soggy mess. Kitchen foil, waxed paper or plastic tubs will protect the specimens. Before moving on, try to pinpoint the location of the find (GPS helps) and note the habitat, e.g. 'among moss on a slope' or 'growing from a beech stump'. The identification of associated trees or other plants may require a leaf or bark sample.

The feature that is most useful for the identification of any fungus, and especially for mushrooms and toadstools, is the colour of its spore print. A spore print is obtained by placing the fruitbody, gill (or tube) face-down, on a piece of glass or white paper and leaving it for up to 12 hours. Cover the fruitbody to prevent it drying out and be aware that white spores may need to be searched for on white paper; however, coloured paper may distort the spore colour. The true colour is best observed from a thick deposit of the spores. Try to distinguish different shades; brown may not be enough. The difference between a rusty-brown or purple–brown spore print will help to narrow down the group to which the specimen belongs.

Good photographs (from above and below) of the fresh specimen can be useful, but a sketch using crayons or watercolour is often better. Remember to indicate the scale as size may be important. The colour of the spore print (if produced) should be included. At this point it should be possible to identify the specimen, at least to its genus, using one of several identification books aimed at the general public (see details on page 204). If this is not possible and an unusual find is suspected, a dried sample will be required to back up any photographs, drawings and notes. Unless it is very large (when the fruitbody will need to be sliced), dry the whole specimen above a radiator or another heat source.

The next course of action is to take the specimen to a member of a local fungus group (see page 204) or enquire whether any nearby museum has a fungus expert on the staff. If all else fails the dried specimen, along with the details outlined above, can be sent to The Mycology Section, Jodrell Laboratory, Royal Botanic Gardens, Kew, Richmond, Surrey TW9 3AB. Remember to enclose a stamped addressed envelope to ensure a reply.

In the autumn of 1998 I was teaching an adult education evening class in Sheffield on Mushrooms and Toadstools. As usual, many of the participants came to the class bearing fungi that they wanted naming. Towards the end of the course, in early December, when the supply of specimens had tailed off, a class member called Dave Buckle arrived with what looked like a deflated, orange–pink squash ball. As I had not seen anything quite like it in any of the identification books I sent it off to Kew along with a note to the effect that it had been found by Mr Buckle among damp soil on a path near Knaresborough.

The immediate reply from Brian Spooner informed me that the strange find was an ascomycete relative of the truffles called *Paurocotylis pila*. The fungus is native to New Zealand and was first recorded in Britain from nearby Nottinghamshire, also in December, in 1973. The earliest Yorkshire record known to Kew was in 1990, and it has since been found in several Scottish locations, including the Orkney Islands. All the evidence indicates that it is spreading. It may have been originally introduced from the southern hemisphere along with garden plants brought in by boat or plane, but its subsequent spread appears to involve more mundane forms of transport. The first Sheffield record turned up less than 2 years after Dave's Knaresborough find. It was discovered growing at the edge of a track that had recently been renovated by a group called Sheffield Environmental Training; the same organisation that had arranged the visit to Knaresborough where Dave had made his original find.

New records are turning up in other habitats, not least those associated with tropical and subtropical plants grown in greenhouses and conservatories. During the past 20 years some of the most exciting new records have come from a relatively new habitat, surfaces covered with woodchip. For those wishing to find mushroom species that may not yet feature in the identification books, the story of mushrooms and woodchips is related in Chapter Eleven.

Climate Change

On the last day of June 2007 I was walking, with my wife Jean, around the reservoirs that feed the fountains and waterworks of the Derbyshire gardens at Chatsworth. As we came to an area of mature birch trees Jean went off in search of fly agarics (*Amanita muscaria*). 'I think you are being a bit optimistic', I said, 'they rarely fruit before September'. Minutes later Jean pointed triumphantly to the white-spotted, red cap that was pushing through the soil. One swallow does not make a summer, but this first fruiting date for fly agaric was nearly 2 months earlier than local 'first' records collected during the 1970s.

With the growing reality of climate change, there have been frequent media reports indicating that the first flowering date of some of our common spring flowers is, on average, many days earlier than records from 40 or 50 years ago. The records of first flowering dates made by Victorian naturalists has enabled comparisons to be made over a time-scale as long as 150 years. At the other end of the season, many British deciduous trees are keeping their leaves well into November; the average date of leaf fall is getting later. Such records have led to a growing interest in phenology, the study of the seasonal timing of life-cycle events such as the deposition of frog spawn.

Anecdotal evidence that the fruiting season for some fungi is both starting earlier and finishing later is supported once again by my own observations of fly agaric. Since the early 1990s I have featured on numerous television programmes about Christmas, with particular reference to a link between Father Christmas and the red and white fly agaric (see page 149). In the *Gem Mushroom* book first published in 1996, I noted that the season for fly agaric was 'late summer to early winter', finishing by the end of November. This meant that fruiting had finished before I was filmed for the Christmas programmes and I had to make do with models. In 2006, when filming for the Christmas sequence of *Castle in the Country*, I was able to use real fly agarics for the first time; they carried on fruiting well into December that year.

Unlike the long sequence of records made by thousands of amateur botanists and ornithologists (listening for the first cuckoo), it is only recently, with the formation of more county fungus groups, that there have been sufficient, reliable, annual fungal records from which first and last fruiting dates for a local area can be ascertained. Two

FACING PAGE:
Fly agaric *Amanita muscaria*

members of the Salisbury and District Natural History Society ensured that for part of south Wiltshire and the New Forest there would be fungal records going back to the 1950s. Ted Gange and Jim Hindley documented their sightings of over 1,000 different species and over the years built up some 55,000 dated records which have recently been analysed by, among others, Ted's son Alan.

Of the spring fruiting mushrooms, the average first fruiting date for morel (*Morchella esculenta*) in the 1950s, in their area, was 13th May. By 2006 the average had moved to 3rd April, some 40 days earlier. Earlier fruiting was found to be closely linked to a significant increase in average February temperatures over the same period. St George's Mushroom (*Calocybe gambosa*) first appeared around 17th May in the 1970s, but by the 2000s it was averaging 22nd April, the day before St George's Day. Work with other species has shown that many fungi that previously fruited in autumn now also fruit in spring. Fairy ring champignon (*Marasmius oreades*) rarely appeared before September in the 1950s, but recent records show that it now starts fruiting as early as June. Other autumn fruiters (such as fly agaric) have been extending their fruiting season by starting earlier in the summer and ending much later. From an average autumn fruiting season of 33 days in the 1950s, the season for some species has lengthened to as much as 75 days. These changes are mirrored by a 50 year decline in the frequency and severity of pre-Christmas frosts in that part of southern England.

Many of these seasonal changes in fungal fruiting times are much greater than those recorded for flowering plants. The longer fruiting periods of many fungi are probably indicative of increased vegetative activity. It has been calculated that compost heaps are now rotting (largely thanks to fungi) at twice the rate they did 50 years ago. It has also been found that fungal species that decay wood and leaf litter are doing so at an enhanced rate. This means that trees (and other plants) should be growing more quickly owing to the greater availability of nutrients resulting from increased fungal recycling. On a more prosaic level, mushroom hunters need to adjust their diaries to take account of the changing season of availability of many edible species.

Climate change has also resulted in more extremes of weather, as exemplified by the very heavy rainfall and associated flooding in the summer of 2007. Such extremes have less effect on the timing of fungal fruitbodies, but they do influence the numbers. The abnormally wet June and July produced a wonderful harvest of truffles in many parts of southern Britain, proving that every cloud has a silver lining.

FACING PAGE:
St George's mushroom – *Calocybe gambosa*

The Names they are a-Changing

In former times scientists had a working knowledge of classical Greek and Latin; in fact, Latin was the international means of communication between scientists of different countries. Up to about the year 1700 most books on learned subjects were written in Latin. For this reason, botanists, who also studied fungi, devised names of plants and fungi that were based on Latin (or Greek). Unfortunately, these names also attempted to describe the organism, with the result that the scientific name often ran to a long sentence; hardly user friendly even to someone with a classical education. From the era of the Ancient Greeks similar species were grouped together and the names of related species started with the same word, what we now call the genus name. For fungi the genus names were often derived more from Greek than from Latin roots. The long-winded problem arose when separating similar species in the same genus by including long descriptions as part of the specific name.

By the 18th century, following the flowering of science, the number of described species of plants and fungi in Europe had grown enormously. At the same time organisms new to Western science were being brought back from many different parts of the world. It took the genius of Linnaeus to come up with a scientific naming system that standardised Latin names and saved both paper and effort. What he realised was that the name of a plant (and in his day fungi were usually included with the plants) did not need to include a description. Linnaeus introduced what has become known as the binomial system, where the scientific name consists of only two words, the first being the genus name, the second signifying the species.

The binomial system was adopted for the scientific names of fungi. Look up the scientific name of field mushroom and it will appear as *Agaricus campestris*, by convention written in italics, with the first letter of the genus name in upper case and that of the species name in lower case. The second word, known as the specific epithet, is often descriptive or gives a reference to the habitat, as in *Agaricus silvicola* (from Latin *silvanus*, situated in a wood), the wood mushroom.

By the end of the 19th century there had been an even greater increase in the number

FACING PAGE:
The prince –
Agaricus augustus

of fungal species described in Europe, but by this time the binomial system for both plants and fungi was running into problems. Some species had been given different names by different botanists, while two or more species were frequently given the same binomial name. To help sort out the problems, the first day of the 20th century saw the implementation of a new international code to be followed in the naming of new plant and fungal species and to sort out previous duplications.

On the plant side the correct name was deemed to be the one first used by Linnaeus in 1753 or the earliest subsequent date that the plant was first named. For fungi this starting date was put at 1821. This anomaly caused more problems in the naming of fungi and in 1981 the date for the first correct name for fungi was put back to 1753, in line with the plants, but with exceptions for names given by Fries and Persoon (see page 21). This change has resulted in some recent name changes. Other problems necessitated the need for new genera. If the genus *Agaricus*, as first used by Fries, had not been split into numerous other genera there would now be over 4,000 species of *Agaricus*, far too many to assist with their accurate identification.

With the advent of chemical and genetic analysis, some species previously thought to be similar enough on morphological grounds to be placed in the same genus were found not to be closely related, resulting in species being moved to a different genus and requiring a name change. This has been the case with many fungi in the past 30 years. Frustratingly, this can make research into a particular species difficult as it may have undergone several changes of name. It is also difficult when comparing different books about mushrooms as some authors will be more up to date than others.

I was recently reading about an edible mushroom in a book published in 1894. The scientific name was given as *Agaricus prunulus*, a name dating back to 1772 and no longer used. Fortunately, the book mentioned an alternative name, *Clitopilus prunulus*, which had first been used in 1871. As it happens this is the name that is still used today and so I could relate to the species being described. Beside the scientific names was a common name, 'plum mushroom'; a name no longer to be found in modern books, which refer to it as the miller. Unlike flowering plants and birds, the majority of fungi were not given English names, the exceptions being those that were good to eat, highly poisonous or had a use (medicinal or otherwise).

FACING PAGE:
The miller – *Clitopilus prunulus*

Scientists have long decried the use of common names in all areas of natural history as being a bar to international understanding, but most amateur naturalists find common

names much easier to remember and less daunting than scientific names. As a result, many 'common' names were hurriedly made up for inclusion in books aimed at the general public, despite such names not necessarily being part of existing folklore. The problem with genuine common names was that different English names arose for the same mushroom in different parts of Britain, and while many fungi had no common name, others had as many as five or six.

In the 1960s the British Mycological Society produced a list of suggested common names for just 200 species. Many of these names caught on, especially as they were used in various field guides, most notably one by Roger Phillips, published in 1981. Even so, nearly 50% of the names did not pass into common usage. By the beginning of the new millennium there had been a huge upsurge in public interest in fungi and to encourage this interest a new, much expanded list of English names for about 1,000 species was

Blistered cup (new English name) – *Peziza vesiculosa*, growing on straw

drawn up in a collaborative venture funded by, among others, the British Mycological Society, Plantlife International and English Nature. The *List of Recommended English Names for Fungi* was launched, with much media publicity, in September 2003.

The new list includes about 400 newly created names, while other long-cherished ones have been altered or dropped in an attempt to bring consistency to the list. With very few exceptions most of the new names consist of two words, mirroring the binomial nature of the scientific names. In some cases this has been achieved by joining words, as in the renaming of scarlet wax cap as scarlet waxcap. The old Anglicising of Latin names such as blackening russula has given way to blackening brittlegill, and political correctness has crept in with the renaming of jew's ear (see page 118). The term mushroom has been reserved for members of the modern genus *Agaricus*, and with just a few exceptions only one English name has been included for species that were previously blessed with several common names.

The recent changes to some scientific and common names may prove difficult for those brought up with the older names. The test of the newly recommended common names will be measured by their acceptance by existing mycologists and those who are new to the subject. In the meantime we are faced with not only changes to the scientific names of some well-known species but also lots of new English names. Many years ago my father was responsible for overseeing the change in both radio and television weather forecasts from Fahrenheit to centigrade. The change was not well received by those used to Fahrenheit, but the younger generation brought up with centigrade had no problem. I suspect that the same will be true of the fungus name changes, but only time will tell. Throughout this book I have used the new English and Latin names, but have also included the older, more well-known ones for the sake of old-timers.

Where do Fungi Live?

We can find the answer to this question on the Beatles' classic 1960s' album *Revolver*, where they sang:

Here, there and everywhere.

Although the distribution of larger fungi, especially those referred to as mushrooms and toadstools, is not quite as extensive as it is for many of the less conspicuous, smaller fungi, the range of habitats that include at least some members of the fungal kingdom is enormous. Fungi, unlike plants, cannot make their own organic matter, so their distribution is largely limited by the availability of materials that they can utilise as fungal food. Some habitats, such as woodlands, contain substantial amounts of potentially available organic matter, whereas others, including the world's oceans, are less favourable. Despite this, oceans are far from devoid of fungi, although most of the species that can put up with the saline conditions are microfungi.

The average amateur mycologist, especially one with a culinary interest, concentrates on finding fruitbodies of the larger fungi including the agarics (mushrooms and toadstools), bracket fungi, puffballs and morels. For mycologists, knowledge of the habitat requirements of sought-after species is comparable to the way in which botanists and ornithologists are able to predict which flowers or birds they may find when visiting a particular habitat.

Common species of mushroom and toadstool include those that are relatively catholic in their taste, but also those species that are restricted to a specific food source that is itself widely available. Rare species often demand exacting habitat requirements that are themselves uncommon. Other rare fungi may be limited by environmental factors such as temperature or water availability. In Britain the latter group are frequently at the edge of a wider distribution throughout mainland Europe.

Dung roundhead (*Stropharia semiglobata*) is a very common 'little brown job' that grows on the weathered dung of a wide range of herbivores, including cow, sheep, horse and rabbit. It is found in pastures, heaths and even in woodland. It also grows on land

FACING PAGE:
King Alfred's cakes *Daldinia concentrica*, growing on ash

fertilised with herbivorous dung and on clifftop grassland, where its normal requirement for animal dung is fulfilled by bird guano.

In contrast, the nail fungus (*Poronia punctata*), an ascomycete with fruitbodies that are shaped like a nail or golf tee, only grows on horse dung and is virtually restricted in Britain to the New Forest where it grows on dung of semi-wild ponies. It is one of the fungal species with a UK Biodiversity Action Plan (see page 95). Until the early part of the 20th century horses, their dung and the nail fungus were all common. In the 21st century, even in those parts of Europe, including Britain, where horses are still kept for riding, the fungus is now very rarely found. It appears that the use of additives in horse feedstuffs and the use of artificial fertilisers on the pastures grazed by horses have affected the nature of horse dung, something that has not happened to dung from the less pampered ponies grazing on the largely unimproved land of the New Forest.

Agaric fruitbody emerging through tarmac

Sulphur tuft (*Hypholoma fasciculare*) is one of the commonest toadstools to be found on the decayed wood of tree stumps, fallen trunks and timber used to make path steps or edging for garden borders. It grows on a very wide range of different tree species, both broadleaved and coniferous; just as its substrate is common so is the fungus. As the common name implies, it grows in dense tufts and, when young, has a sulphur-yellow cap, stem and gills, the latter turning purplish-brown as the spores mature. Sadly, this very frequent fungus is not edible as it has a very bitter taste, comparable to quinine.

Birch polypore (*Piptoporus betulinus*) is nearly as common as sulphur tuft, despite being restricted to birch trees. This is because birch trees are very common in Britain and the fungus, which is a parasite on living trees, can continue to live as a saprophyte on dead ones. In contrast, oak polypore (*Piptoporus quercinus*) is rare enough to need protection in a manner similar to that for the nail fungus. It grows on dead wood in the trunks of veteran oaks, usually ancient deer park or forest trees (often over 400 years old) that were formerly pollarded. Unlike young birches, the number of veteran oaks is very limited and so too, as a result, is the oak polypore.

The distribution and frequency of many woodland fungi are strongly influenced by their need for very specific habitats. Fungi that form mycorrhizal associations with tree roots (see Chapter Ten) often do so with only one or a limited number of tree species. Examples include the larch bolete (*Suillus grevillei*), associated with larch trees, and beech milkcap (*Lactarius blennius*), which is only rarely found away from beech trees. Some species obtain their food from tree fruits, including ear pick fungus (*Auriscalpium vulgare*), a small toadstool that grows only on partially buried pine cones. Other more common fungi feed on the discarded leaf litter that is a feature of deciduous woodland. Typical of these is wood woollyfoot (*Collybia peronata*).

Larch bolete – *Suillus grevillei*

Fungi of grassland communities include field mushroom (*Agaricus campestris*) and species such as yellow fieldcap, previously known as egg-yolk fungus (*Bolbitius titubans*, was *B. vitellinus*), which feed on decayed grass leaves, dung and straw. Some 50 species of waxcap (*Hygrocybe* spp.) are largely restricted to old, unlimed, grazed pasture that has not had inorganic fertiliser added. This is a habitat whose area has declined by over 90% since 1930. Mown, unfertilised old lawns and even some cemeteries are also homes for waxcaps and other species that are unable to compete in grassland where lime and inorganic fertilisers have been applied.

Other habitats that include fungi specific to them include coastal dune systems, where such rarities as the dune stinkhorn (*Phallus hadriani*) and dune mushroom (*Agaricus devoniensis*) are to be found. The fruitbodies of dune mushroom develop under the sand, only pushing through as the spores mature; possibly a strategy to cut down on water loss in what is a very dry environment.

A strange group of fungi grows on burnt ground associated with bonfires, forest fires and the controlled or accidental burning of heather moorland. Such 'phoenicoid' fungi (as in phoenix-like, literally arising from the ashes) include the beautiful tiger's eye or brown goblet (*Coltricia perennis*), a bracket fungus with a mushroom shape that is occasionally used in florists' displays. Tiger's eye also grows in other sites, especially on sandy, acidic soil. In contrast bonfire scalycap (*Pholiota highlandensis*), a brown toadstool, is restricted to fire sites in either woodland or heathland. Despite this limitation it is common and widespread, as are fire sites. It is often found with bonfire inkcap (*Coprinus jonesii*), which is only rarely found away from burnt ground. Several cup or disc-like ascomycete fungi inhabit fire sites, where the ground may be covered with their fruitbodies. One of these is the stalked bonfire cup (*Geopixis carbonaria*).

Geopixis is occasionally found protruding from the mortar of garden walls or emerging from damp plaster inside houses. Both these sites are very alkaline (they have a high pH) because of their lime content. The fresh ash resulting from wood or heathland fires is also extremely alkaline, one reason why fresh ash should not be used as a garden mulch. Very few fungi or plants can thrive in such conditions, but it appears that many phoenicoid fungi are adapted to and even thrive in an environment that is toxic to other species.

A relative of *Geopixis* is even more at home in our homes. Cellar cup (*Peziza cerea*) produces clumps of delicate, pale buff-coloured, cup-shaped fruitbodies up to 3–4 cm across. It grows on damp mortar or earth in moist cellars and erupts from rotting sandbags (an increasingly common habitat in flood-prone areas). It is famous for its association with toilets, where the moist conditions of gentlemen's urinals, or on a wall or carpet soaked by a leaking cistern may result in large numbers of the fruitbodies. Fortunately, cellar cup does little damage and may even be a useful indicator of the damp conditions on which it thrives. Such conditions may provide a foothold for a much more serious household fungus and one that is not found outside any artificial habitat in Britain; dry rot (*Serpula lacrymans*) (see Chapter Twenty-one).

Gardens, along with parks, playing fields and churchyards, provide important urban sites for mushrooms and toadstools. Mycorrhizal species (see page 53) that obtain their food from tree roots are common in gardens and parks, and even on pavements. Earthballs (*Scleroderma* spp.) frequently burst through tarmac or thrust up between paving stones. Toadstools that are mycorrhizal with garden trees include a range of boletes, especially red cracking bolete (*Boletus chrysenteron*) and species of milkcap (*Lactarius*) and brittlegill (*Russula*). Not all of these require mature trees; woolly milkcap (*Lactarius torminosus*) may form fairy rings around birch trees that are no more than 10 years old.

Parasitic fungi species that parasitise and kill both trees and shrubs have more serious consequences for gardeners and park keepers. One such toadstool is honey fungus, which in older books went under the name *Armillaria mellea* and whose destructive nature is outlined in Chapter Twenty-two. Lawns are home to many species known as 'little brown jobs', of which brown mottlegill or hay cap (*Panaeolina foenisecii*) is the most common. This poisonous toadstool is not infrequently devoured by inquisitive young children and also by dogs, but the outcome is rarely serious, if worrying for parents and pet owners. I was pleased to find magic mushroom (*Psilocybe semilanceata*) growing on my own back lawn (see page 143), but lawn fanatics, along with bowling and golf green keepers are less enamoured of fairy ring fungus (*Marasmius oreades*), which often disfigures the turf on which it grows (see page 63).

As the organic, recycling movement has spread so the garden compost heap has made a comeback. Microfungi and bacteria are responsible for the breakdown of organic waste, a process that may cause the compost to reach temperatures as high as 60°C. Such conditions are only tolerated by thermophilic (heat-loving) toadstools including some species of inkcap (*Coprinus* spp.). Older heaps are occasionally colonised by wood blewit (*Lepista nuda*), whose mauve-gilled fruitbodies are edible and excellent; a bonus for the organic gardener. The use of woodchip on paths and as a garden mulch has 'mushroomed' in the past 20 years, bringing with it a range of toadstools not previously encountered in gardens or anywhere else in Britain (see page 59). Equally, the growing of exotic plants in heated greenhouses and conservatories has resulted in increased sightings of tropical fungi in Britain. Among the most conspicuous of these is plantpot dapperling or yellow parasol (*Leucocoprinus birnbaumii*), a bell-shaped little toadstool recognised by its bright yellow, scurfy cap with a distinctly grooved margin. Its first European record, in the early part of the 19th century, was in Prague Botanic Garden.

Another relatively new habitat has provided a novel home for a previously unusual British fungus. This is the very beautiful split-gill (*Schizophyllum commune*). Looking like a small furry bracket fungus from above, the underside reveals a fan-like, coralloid mass of branching gills. Most British records up until the middle of the 20th century came

Wood blewit – *Lepista nuda*

from south-eastern England, where it grows on fallen wood (especially beech) exposed to the sun. By the start of the 21st century I had begun to find it in the Peak District, possibly an example of a move northwards under the influence of climate change. As a thermophilic species it is more common in tropical regions, but it has now found a new home in Britain; plastic-wrapped bales of hay. The mycelium grows on the warm contents of the bags and its fruitbodies emerge through the plastic lining.

In 2002 the same fungus made headlines with its ability to grow in another warm place: the human body. 'Fatal Fungus that Preys on Humans' was the title for one newspaper story. The fungus mycelium has been found to cause mouth ulcers and toenail infections; hardly fatal, but the fungus can be much more of a problem for people suffering from a suppressed immune system, including those infected with HIV or anyone taking immunosuppressant drugs.

Given that, unlike green plants, mushrooms and toadstools do not require light for the maintenance of their nutrition, it should come as no surprise that caves and old mines have been, and still are, used to grow edible mushrooms. In France the ordinary white mushrooms are still known as Paris mushrooms from the time when they were only cultivated in old mines beneath Paris. A number of fungi occur naturally in such habitats, including some microfungi that are not found anywhere else. Of the larger fungi growing in old mines, some species attack wooden pit props, such as the mine fungus (*Antrodia vaillantii*), a bracket fungus that also rots wooden greenhouses and has even been recorded growing on wet coke. Dry rot (*Serpula lacrymans*) also occurs in mines, where it may assume unusual growth forms (see page 71).

A small number of toadstools obtain their food by growing on, or in close proximity with, the fruitbodies of other fungi. Parasitic bolete (*Pseudoboletus parasiticus*) is a small yellow–brown-capped bolete that is occasionally found growing from the base of fruitbodies of common earthball (*Scleroderma citrinum*). As its name implies, it has long been presumed to be parasitic on the earthball, but some researchers believe that it only requires the presence of the earthball to stimulate fruiting and is not a parasite. Similar doubts surround the rare piggyback rosegill (*Volvariella surrecta*), which I have only seen once in the past 30 years when I found clusters of the toadstool emerging from the decaying remains of some clouded agarics (*Clitocybe nebularis*). The rosegill could be a parasite or live only on the dead fruitbodies of clouded agaric; it has never been found in any other situation. The well-known yellow brain (*Tremella mesenterica*), a jelly fungus that brightens old stems of gorse and other shrubs through the winter, has now been found to be parasitic on the mycelium of another fungus within the twig. Life is not always what it seems.

Microfungi occupy many more habitats than do the larger mushrooms and toadstools. These include both fresh and salt water. British examples of the former that have come to public attention are fish moulds, one of which causes black patches and the untimely death of many a pet goldfish, and another which results in the death of salmon. Fungi also attack insects, including house flies, and the honeycomb of hive bees. Plant parasites include the rust fungi which, along with mildews and related 'moulds', cause immense damage in both horticulture and agriculture. Microfungi cause food spoilage and also kill trees, although the fungus that has left its mark by killing elm trees is in fact an ascomycete, but with tiny fruitbodies that are rarely seen (see Chapter Twenty-one).

Humans provide an unwelcome home for fungi in the form of ringworm and thrush. Some fungi have even caused eye infections in contact lens solutions. Species of *Malassezia*, tiny yeast-like fungi, are present on our skin where they feed on the oily products of our sebaceous glands. These fungi can cause dermatitis and more commonly the shedding of skin flakes; so even dandruff can be blamed on fungi. Other microfungi result in the brown foxing seen in old books, the etching of the glass in cameras and field glasses, and the spoiling of the surface of CDs.

Perhaps most intriguing of all is the fungus that 'eats' jet and diesel fuel. Oil is, of course, an organic material, being composed of the long-dead remains of marine organisms, so it should come as no surprise that a range of microfungi has been detected in oil-based fuels. The most important of these is the creosote fungus *Amorphotheca resinae*, which not only breaks down creosote (which has been used as a preservative against fungi) but can also feed on jet fuel (kerosene) as long as at least a little water (ten parts of water per million of fuel is enough) is available. Empty tanks are vulnerable to condensation in humid conditions and this can provide the necessary water. High-flying aircraft experience very low temperatures, but the creosote fungus can put up with temperatures down to –25°C. The greatest danger to planes and their passengers comes from the fungal mycelium, which may block filters and small pipes, thus preventing fuel flow to an engine.

As with all fungi, preventing the initial infection is one way of limiting damage. Many years ago I was told a story by someone who had worked for the RAF. He recounted a big NATO exercise involving jet planes from different countries which, as part of the training, were refuelled in mid-air from special tanker planes. Only later was it discovered that one tanker plane was infected with creosote fungus and, in a manner analogous to the transmission of sexual disease, the fungus had been passed on in the refuelling process. Expensive decontamination was required. The same fungus can also live on diesel (contaminated with water), resulting in fuel blockage in cars and lorries. Fungi really are 'Here, there and everywhere'.

Bread mould – *Rhizopus stolonifera*, scanning electron micrograph of a sporangium

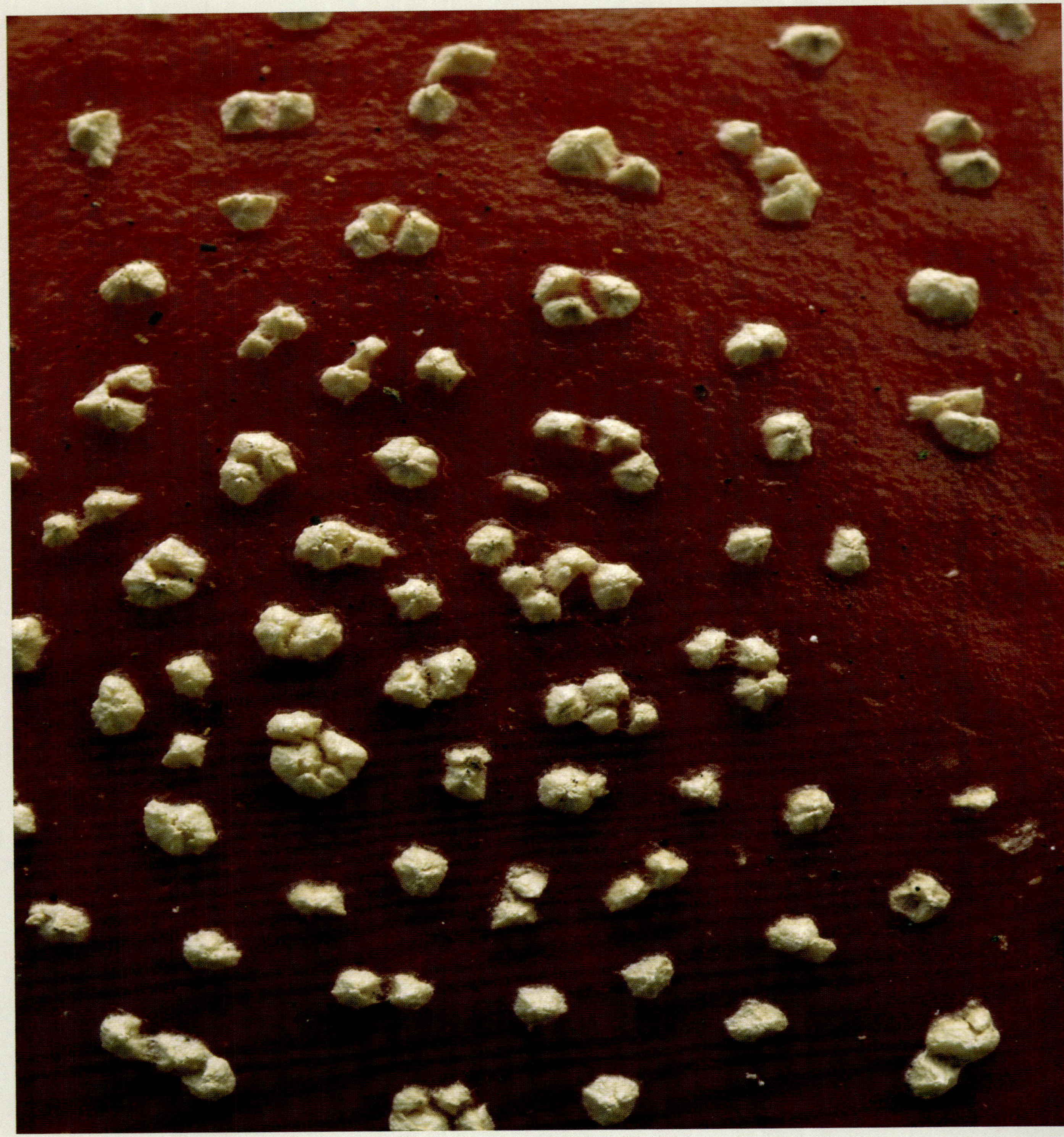

Getting to the Root of the Matter

As an undergraduate, over 40 years ago, I learnt about the way in which plants absorb water and nutrients through their roots. Descriptions of the chemical and physical processes involved were accompanied by pictures of root hairs and estimates of their phenomenal surface area. No mention was made of fungi. In separate lectures I learnt that some species of mushroom and toadstool formed intimate relationships with the roots of trees.

Some of the earliest work on the link between trees and fungi was initiated in the 1880s. It followed a request by the Prussian Minister for Agriculture, Lands and Forests for research into the commercial growing of truffles. A.B. Frank examined tree rootlets and observed their associated sheath of fungal threads. He called the association a mycorrhiza [from the Greek *mykes*, (Latin *mycos*) fungus, and *rhiza*, root].

A mycorrhiza is now defined as a symbiotic relationship (in that usually both plant and fungus benefit) in which the mycelium of a fungus supplies soil-derived nutrients to a plant root. In return the fungus is supplied with sugars manufactured by the plant. About 40% of the world's woodland mushrooms and toadstools are believed to be involved in mycorrhizal relationships with trees. However, trees are not the only plants involved and recent research has estimated that over 90% of plant species in the world develop fungus roots through which nutrients and water are absorbed.

Given the Greek/Latin basis of the word mycorrhiza, the plural was originally written as mycorrhizae; a term I remember using in my student days. In the modern world it appears that mycorrhizae have been replaced by mycorrhizas, a reversal of the Victorian pedantry that fought against funguses in favour of fungi as the plural of fungus. More confusing still is the use of mycorrhiza to imply the plural; a cause of sleep loss only alleviated by the counting of sheeps.

Only 3% of the world's plant species produce sheathing mycorrhizas of the type first studied in the 19th century and now termed ectomycorrhizas (Greek *ektos*, outside). Among these plants are many common trees (and some woody shrubs) of temperate regions, while the fungal partners include well-known mushrooms and toadstools.

FACING PAGE:
Close up of fly agaric – *Amanita muscaria*, a common mycorrhizal fungus

Ectomycorrhizas are commonly associated with trees such as oak, beech, birch, willow, alder and hazel, together with conifers including pine, larch and spruce. Tree species rarely, or never, forming ectomycorrhizas include sycamore, ash, elm, rowan and hawthorn; a major reason why the ground under these trees is less productive for mushroom hunters.

Fungi that form ectomycorrhizas with only one, or a small number of tree species include edible species of truffle, chanterelle, bolete, milkcap and hedgehog mushroom along with toadstools such as death cap (*Amanita phalloides*), fly agaric (*Amanita muscaria*) and brown rollrim (*Paxillus involutus*). A tree's roots may cover an area that is much greater than its canopy and this can result in the production of fruitbodies of ectomycorrhizal fungi as far as 100 m from their host's trunk; the connection is not always obvious. Confusingly, the hyphae of some ectomycorrhizal fungi obtain their nutrients from fallen leaf litter rather than via plant roots. Woodland toadstools occurring on areas of chalk grassland where there are no trees have been shown to form mycorrhizas with rock-roses, which are small woody shrubs. While leading a group of botanists to see the marsh helleborine orchid in the wet dune slacks near Harlech I was fascinated to observe several large fruitbodies of brown rollrim (*Paxillus involutus*) towering above the creeping willow with which they had formed a mycorrhizal association; an Alice in Wonderland wood where the mushrooms were bigger than the trees.

The importance of ectomycorrhizas lies in their influence on the growth of the trees that are involved. It is still a commonly held fallacy that a tree 'infected' with toadstools, appearing from the ground around it, will be less healthy than an uninfected one. That there is a cost to the tree is shown by research indicating that as much as 25% of the host's photosynthetic products, mostly in the form of glucose and fructose, pass to the fungus, but what the tree gains will often outweigh this drain on its carbohydrates. Plant roots only absorb a small percentage of soil-based nitrogen and phosphorus, two nutrients essential for plant growth. Fungus roots which develop long-lived side branches, increase this absorption by up to 50-fold, especially in poor soil areas. The implications for forestry are enormous. For many years tree seedlings have been inoculated with ectomycorrhizal fungi before being transferred to new plantations on land that has not previously grown trees. The growth rates of such trees have been shown to be up to twice those of non-inoculated trees that have not formed beneficial fungus roots.

FACING PAGE:
Brown rollrim –
Paxillus involutus

Ironically, the addition of inorganic fertilisers in poor soil regions used for forestry may have a detrimental effect on the mycorrhizas with the result that *less* nutrient reaches the trees.

Before Frank's pioneering work, similar, short stubby rootlets, encased in a matted sheath, had been observed by American scientists trying to determine how 'parasitic' Indian pipe plants (which lack the green pigment chlorophyll and thus the ability to manufacture sugars) obtained their nutrients. In Britain the bird's nest orchid, a woodland plant that also lacks chlorophyll, has been shown to form a parasitic relationship with a nearby existing tree/fungus mycorrhizal association. Bird's nest describes the appearance of the orchid/fungus/tree roots, a feature that remains hidden underground.

Trees rarely or never forming ectomycorrhizas include holly, yew and field maple, along with introductions such as horse chestnut and London plane. Such trees and a very wide range of shrubs and non-woody plants (herbs) form endomycorrhizas in which the fungal partner invades the root cells of the plant. The fungi that are involved belong to a group known as the Glomales. These differ from mushrooms and toadstools in that their hyphae lack cross-walls and very few species produce large fruitbodies. Partly for this reason, VA (vesicular–arbuscular) mycorrhizas, as they are now known, were largely ignored until the 1970s.

It is now becoming apparent that VA mycorrhizas aid growth in trees that do not benefit from ectomycorrhizas. Discussing the implications of this, a leading researcher in the field observed 'If a tree is not mycorrhizal, it is a dead tree'. VA mycorrhizas are also found in most herbaceous plants, including grasses and cereals. Here too the result is increased absorption of nitrogen and phosphorus by the plants. The transportation of phosphorus by fungal mycelia has been observed at rates as high as 0.5 m per hour; a very efficient distribution network. This may necessitate a review of agricultural practices. The cultivation of soil destroys the mycelia that forms part of the beneficial mycorrhizas, not to mention the negative effects on the fungal partners of inorganic fertiliser additions.

VA mycorrhizas are also found in mosses and ferns. Fossil relatives of the ferns, complete with fungus roots, have been found in rock deposits from 400 million years ago. It is probable that mycorrhizas helped plants to colonise the land and thus played an important role in the evolution of higher plants.

In addition to increased nutrient absorption, plants benefit from mycorrhizas through an increased uptake of water. The ability of many plants to cope with climate change may be dependent on the presence of healthy mycorrhizas. Successful plant colonisation of soils of unusually high or low acidity, a common feature of land reclaimed after mining or industrial activity, is also dependent on the beneficial results of mycorrhizas. Additionally, mycorrhizas appear to give plants some protection from pathogenic fungi and parasitic nematodes.

Products which include the spores of 'friendly mycorrhizal fungi' are now being advertised, aimed at gardeners. Plants that appear never to form any mycorrhizas include rushes and, more importantly for the gardener, members of the cabbage family. One group of plants, including heathers, rhododendrons, azaleas, bilberries and cranberries, forms a third category of mycorrhizas in which the fungal partner is an ascomycete (see page 26) with tiny cup-shaped fruitbodies. Fungus roots so formed enable such species to grow in very acidic soils and may prevent the growth of ectomycorrhizal tree species; one reason for the slow growth rates achieved by heathland forestry plantations.

Orchids form endomycorrhizas, typically with species of microfungi, many of which parasitise and kill other plants. The seeds of orchids, unlike those of most flowering plants, are so tiny that they are unable to supply the developing seedling with enough food before the young plant is able to make its own. At a very early stage a germinating orchid seed is invaded by fungal hyphae which provide sufficient food for the orchid's growth and development. Even after the plant is producing photosynthetic materials of its own, most orchids maintain their fungal association, but continue to give little or nothing to the fungus. For this reason orchid mycorrhizas are not truly symbiotic as the orchid is actually parasitic on the fungus. Many orchid flowers are now grown commercially by supplying food in a nutrient medium to germinating seeds or cuttings (or plants grown from tissue culture), thus bypassing the need for any fungal relationship.

Mushrooms and Woodchips

The above heading is not taken from an all-day breakfast menu, but reflects the significance of a novel habitat that has become increasingly common in Britain since the mid-1980s. The new habitat consists of layers of woodchip, spread on garden beds, paths and children's play areas, where the mulch helps to suppress weeds and maintain soil moisture. The standard material available from garden centres should strictly be called barkchips as it is usually sourced from flaked pine bark and contains no woody material. Woodchip is widely available as a waste product resulting from tree-surgery and forestry work and consists of a mixture containing both heartwood and bark, typically from deciduous trees and shrubs. It appears that hardwood woodchip attracts a much more diverse fungal flora than coniferous barkchip.

The popularity of woodchip has resulted in part from its cheapness. Contractors previously had to remove trees and large branches and pay to dispose of these in landfill sites. In contrast, chipped material can be easily stored and sold, resulting in income rather than expenditure. Use of woodchip mulch reduces the use of weedkillers and expensive labour. Among the first clients to use woodchip mulch were councils and other landowners who used it in parks and display beds. London sites include Kew Gardens and Buckingham Palace. Given that many woodland mushrooms are wood-rotting species we should perhaps have anticipated one consequence of the equivalent of putting porridge out for bears. To date nearly 200 species of larger fungi have been recorded on woodchip; a list that is still growing.

Among our native mushrooms those that have readily colonised layers of woodchip include the fascinating bird's-nest fungi (*Cyathus* spp.), whose tiny cup-shaped fruit-bodies contain egg-like spore packets. Another is the beautiful, black-spored magpie inkcap (*Coprinus picaceus*). Other black-spored species that have frequently been found on woodchip include the crumblecaps (species of *Psathyrella*). Of greater interest to the gastronomic mushroom hunter has been the spread of the highly prized morels (various species of *Morchella*) into ground mulched with woodchips. These ascomycete fungi look like brains on stalks and are spring-fruiting mushrooms that now appear many

FACING PAGE:
Magpie inkcap – *Coprinus picaceus*

Common morel – *Morchella esculenta*

weeks earlier than they did 50 years ago (see page 34). This appears to be related to climate change, but could also reflect an increase of records from urban garden sites which are generally several degrees warmer than the surrounding countryside.

My first indication of this trend came in the mid-1980s when I was delighted to find a group of common morels (*Morchella esculenta*), on a woodchip-mulched rose bed in Cambridge Botanic Gardens. Twenty years later a student presented me with a collection of the black morel, known in North America as the urban morel (*Morchella elata*). These had appeared on the heavily woodchipped region of his workplace car park in Wiltshire. The area had been totally re-landscaped less than 18 months before the morels started to appear. Given the high price of morels this should be an added incentive for all mycophilic gardeners to apply a deep layer of woodchip. Beware false morel (*Gyromitra esculenta*), which despite its Latin name can prove fatal. It is also a spring fruiter and is increasingly turning up on mulched beds.

The woodchip habitat has also become home to a number of previously very rare species and indeed to species that had not been found in Britain before. Of the former, one of the most conspicuous is redlead roundhead (*Stropharia aurantiaca*) a mushroom with a bright, orange–red convex cap and purple–brown spores that was, until the 1980s, a rare fungus of rotting sawdust piles. In the past 20 years it has become both frequent and widespread, especially on piles of woodchip, where it often fruits in large numbers. It is thought to be native to Australia, but when and how it was introduced to Britain is not known. It is now spreading in four different continents.

In the summer of 2006 my daily dog walk took me passed a large pile of woodchip, the result of earlier tree surgery. To my surprise it became festooned with several hundred large, brown-capped mushrooms which I did not recognise and could not find in any book. It turned out to be *Agrocybe rivulosa*, a species new to science when it was discovered in the Netherlands in 2003. Its first British record, in 2004, was from a garden woodchip pile in Leek, not far from Sheffield. It is now spreading (even on sycamore woodchip) in much the same way as the redlead roundhead. It awaits a common name as it was not known in Britain when the list of suggested names (page 37) was drawn up.

Another *Agrocybe* species originally found in France, growing on old plum stones, turned up in Kew Gardens, from where it has started spreading on mulched flowerbeds. In 1998 large troops of a small, black-spored mushroom were discovered in the grounds of Buckingham Palace, on flowerbeds mulched with woodchip. *Panaeolus atrobalteatus* was the name given to what turned out to be a previously unknown species; perhaps it should be called the gardenparty mottlegill? Some species of *Panaeolus* are hallucinogenic, as are many of their more infamous relatives in the genus *Psilocybe* (see page 143). The native magic mushroom (*Psilocybe semilanceata*) grows in grassland, but several alien species are now colonising woodchip.

Foremost of these is the blueleg brownie (*Psilocybe cyanescens*), a small, gregarious, mealy smelling, wavy brown-capped toadstool which, as its name implies, has a stem (and cap) that discolours blue–green with handling. Blueleg brownie is native to the forests of the north-western USA, where its powerful hallucinogenic properties are well known. Its first British site was in Kew Gardens, where it was collected in 1910 but not described and named until 1946. It has since spread on woodchip mulch to become locally abundant in southern England. One report of a riding track covered with woodchip estimated the number of fruitbodies as in the order of 10,000; more than enough to make the horses fly.

Blueleg brownie is one of a number of species that have spread on woodchip, but are now beginning to colonise more natural habitats. It has been recorded on decaying wood in a number of sites in southern England, including in the New Forest, well away from areas making use of woodchip. For those living in urban areas the fascinating variety of woodchip mushrooms offers a chance to observe new and often colourful mushrooms. Do not expect them all to feature in mushroom guides; they are way ahead of the books.

Of Rings and things

In 1999 a photograph of a fairy ring appeared in the *Fortean Times*, a journal dedicated to supernatural issues. The correspondent put forward suggestions that the 'mysterious circle' was possibly the result of 'Earth energies' or aliens. The latter are believed by many to be responsible for much more intricate designs known as crop circles which have appeared in some profusion over the past 30 years, especially in the cereal fields of Wiltshire. To scientists there has been no mystery associated with fairy rings for over 200 years, but the British public are hardly famous for their scientific knowledge.

In medieval times there was no scientific explanation as to the cause of the dark green rings of grass clearly visible throughout much of the year in grazed grassland (and later in the lawns of country houses and on playing fields), often associated with a racetrack-like circle of short or dead grass. That such rings were briefly festooned with the fruitbodies of mushrooms was recorded, but the fungi were deemed to be a result of the ring rather than its cause.

In medieval Britain the mysterious circles were variously ascribed to the actions of slugs, snails, moles, goats, grazing cattle and toads (a rather tentative link with toadstools), and more especially to fairies, witches and the landing of, not aliens, but bolts of lightning. They were even attributed to the 'exhalations of a fertile subterranean vapour'. Slugs and snails were implicated in the early 18th century writing of Bradley:

> *Garden Snails and Slugs when they couple always make the choice of short grass to creep upon. It is their manner when they generate to take a large compass on the Ground and meet one another. Thus I have seen them creep in a circle for more than half an hour, going over the same ground at least twenty times before they could join, leaving upon the Grass where they crept a viscous shining Matter. So that it may be that Slime, when it putrefies, may produce the Mushrooms we find growing in Circles upon Commons;*

Interestingly, this explanation as to the origin of the racetrack also implies that Bradley believed that mushrooms arose from slime, a belief held by Pliny but discredited in the 17th century by observations of fungal spores. Bradley, in common with the

FACING PAGE:
Woodland fairy ring

photographer mentioned above, was not quite up with the times. Other 18th century authors implicate the mole as the instigator of fairy rings:

> *that at least some of them may be occasioned by the working of Moldwarps (moles) which, however for the most part irregular they may be, yet have a time when perhaps by instinct of nature they may work in circles; as tis certain fallow Deer do in the time of Rutting, treading the same ring for many days together. Indeed the strange fertility of these green Circles … doth argue some extraordinary dung or compost, which he supposes to be the excrement of Moles or Moldwarps.*

The writer of the above attributes the cause of the circle of dead grass to the treading action of a mole. The lush growth of the greener grass ring is the result of the animal's dung. A more ingenious explanation as to the cause of larger fairy rings was recorded by the same author:

> *… from the dung and urine of cattle fed in winter time at the same pout of hay, for their heads meeting at the hay as the centre, and their bodies representing as it were so many radii, has made some imagine that such circles are described by their dung and urine falling always from them in due distance and fertilising the ground in a more than ordinary manner.*

Larger rings were also assumed to be the result of tethered animals such as goats. By walking in a circle at the limit of their tether they would create a circular pathway and the richer grass ring from the action of their dung. Earlier beliefs that toads inhabited the ground encompassed by the rings simply substantiate the link between toads and fairies.

Among the British names for the circles were fairy dances and fairy walls (together with the still common fairy rings), but witches were implicated in the name hag tracks mirrored in the German hexen (witchcraft) rings and the French *ronds de sorcières*. The rings were widely held to be of supernatural origin. Coupled with this was a belief that bad luck would befall any one who stepped within the confines of a fairy ring and that the grass therein was poisonous to grazing animals. Prospero alludes to this in Shakespeare's *The Tempest*:

> *You demi-puppets that*
> *By moonshine do the green sour ringlets make,*
> *Whereof ewe not bites; and you, whose pastime*
> *Is to make midnight mushrooms …*

That lightning strikes might cause the ring of 'burnt' grass was simply an extension of an earlier belief that all mushrooms grew as the result of thunderstorms. Mushrooms are often more frequent in the days following a thunderstorm, but this is not some divine origin but because water is necessary for the expansion of fungal fruitbodies.

Gilbert White, writing in 1780, realised that whatever caused the rings could be transported in turfs brought into his garden and came close to unravelling the mystery when he observed of the rings:

> *Wherever they obtain puff balls abound, the seed of which were doubtless brought in the turf.*

It was left to William Withering, better known for his treatise on the medicinal properties of the foxglove, to make a definite link with *Marasmius oreades* in 1792 (although in his time it was called *Agaricus oreades*) when he wrote:

> *I am satisfied that the bare and brown, or highly clothed and verdant circles, in pasture fields, called Fairy Rings are caused by the growth of this Agaric.*

Fairy ring champignon – *Marasmius oreades*

That Withering proved to be correct is evident in the current common name for *Marasmius oreades*, the fairy ring champignon. While this fungus is the bane of many lawn fanatics it is not the only species whose fruitbodies grow in a ring. Rings are produced by at least 100 British species, of which most are agarics (mushrooms and toadstools) together with some puffball species. Ring-forming fungi include woodland species where tree roots may obfuscate the perfect ring shape and the cryptic effects of leaf litter result in a less obvious spectacle. Several of these form mycorrhizal associations with tree roots and this appears to limit the size of the ring, in contrast to ring-forming species in grassland habitats. Common woodland ring-formers include clouded funnel (*Clitocybe nebularis*), butter cap or greasy tough shank (*Collybia butyracea*) and, most spectacularly, fly agaric (*Amanita muscaria*).

Three different groups of grassland ring-formers have been described, of which the archetype *Marasmius* fits into type I. Here, the ring is clearly visible even in the absence of any fruitbodies and shows as a ring of dead/dying grass sandwiched between rings of darker green grass. Fruitbodies appear in the outer region of the dead zone. As with all ring-forming species the circle of fruitbodies result from the natural growth pattern of fungal threads, known as hyphae, that develop from a germinated fungal spore. The branching hyphae form a disc-shaped waft of tissue (the mycelium) which grows outwards from its perimeter. Under uniform soil conditions it maintains its circular outline much as a mould does on the surface of jam. Just as apple trees produce fruits from the young twigs near the tree's growing edge, so fruitbodies occur close to the perimeter of a fungus mycelium.

As the diameter of the hyphal disc expands at rates of between 20 and 70 cm every year, the hyphae nearer the centre die and release nitrogen, resulting in taller, greener grass. The outer ring of darker green grass marks the growing edge of the fungal mycelium; this is making nitrogen available from the action of its enzymes on organic matter in the soil. The narrow zone of short, brown, dying grass marks an area of prolific mycelial growth which competes with the grass roots for water.

Species such as field mushroom (*Agaricus campestris*), St George's mushroom (*Calocybe gambosa*) and giant puffball (*Calvatia gigantea*) form type II rings which produce circles of stimulated grass and fruitbodies, but lack the brown stunted zone. Many of the colourful waxcaps (*Hygrocybe* spp.) form rings of fruitbodies, with no obvious effect on the grass. Unlike the other types, their presence can only be detected when the fruitbodies are produced. Only *Marasmius*, with its brown ring, is destructive of turf and unsightly. Its elimination from lawns involves the laying of new turf (after sterilisation of the underlying soil) or the use of fungicides.

How Old is a Mushroom?

The fruitbody of an individual field mushroom lasts for no more than 2 weeks and the same is true of most species of mushroom and toadstool. The ephemeral nature of mushrooms has long been remarked on and has even become part of fungal folklore. In general, the typically short-lived fruitbodies have created an impression that fungi themselves are short-lived. This is analogous with the assumption that an apple tree is not very old because its apples are only around for a few months. The longevity of a fruit tree can be clearly seen; the same is not the case for the vegetative part of a mushroom which is hidden out of sight within the soil. Most bracket fungi produce fruitbodies that are much longer lived and some, such as the hoof fungus (*Fomes fomentarius*), develop perennial fruitbodies in which a new layer of spore-bearing tubes is laid down each year. This allows the fruitbody, but not the individual producing it, to be aged.

In addition to any historical evidence substantiating the age of a tree, the annual rings laid down in the wood of its trunk provide an accurate record of its longevity. Can we use comparable techniques to discover the age of the underground mycelium of an individual mushroom? Sadly the answer is no! We can, however, make use of rings of a different kind to provide estimates of the age of some species of mushroom. Fairy rings (see previous chapter) can provide accurate estimations of the age of an individual mycelium.

The 19th century mycologist Reverend Berkeley, writing about fairy rings, commented:

> *These rings are sometimes of very ancient date, and attain enormous dimensions, so as to be distinctly visible on a hill-side from a considerable distance. It is believed that they originate from a single fungus.*

By the 20th century, aerial photography provided further evidence (circles of darker green grass) of large fairy rings, some up to 800 m in diameter. Such large rings are mostly restricted to places such as the South Downs where the grassland has not been ploughed up and has been relatively undisturbed for centuries. I once had the good fortune to find a fairy ring of fruiting giant puffballs (*Calvatia gigantea*) that was over 100 m across. The ring of giants was in permanent pasture land next to an old monastery in Shropshire. I wondered whether the monks had observed a smaller ring: food for thought. They also provided food for my supper.

Observations of fairy rings, especially those made by the fairy ring champignon (*Marasmius oreades*), have been made over successive years in an attempt to measure the average annual increase in diameter of the fruiting ring. As with the growth of trees there are good years and bad years for fungal growth. Fungal growth is dependent on temperature, water and nutrient availability. The rate of increase in the diameter of a ring of *Marasmius* is in the range of 20–70 cm per year. Even if we take the upper figure, rather than an average, this means that a ring of nearly 800 m diameter must have been made by an individual that is at least 1,100 years old (70 cm x 1,100 years = 770 m).

With the exception of some old trees (oaks, limes and yews) this would make an individual fairy ring champignon older than any plant in Britain and certainly far from ephemeral. Other individual fungi are less likely to be so long lived. A fungus that is a tree parasite will usually die when its host is killed. Habitat disturbance such as ploughing will often end the life of individual fungi, and those that live in specialised habitats such as horse droppings will only last as long as their deposit.

For soil-inhabiting fungi that do not form fairy rings it was not possible to detect the extent of an individual's spread and thus attempt to calculate its age, before the development of DNA analysis. The precise sequence of bases in an individual's DNA is unique, and this tagging system is now extensively used in the analysis of hair, skin or other samples to link a person to the scene of a crime. Genetic analysis is also extensively used to resolve taxonomic questions about the evolutionary relationship between different species; those with very similar base patterns are likely to be closely related even if they differ greatly in appearance.

A 1992 paper in *Nature* reported the results of DNA analysis in a population of *Armillaria bulbosa* (now *A. gallica*), the bulbous honey fungus, one of a complex of closely related species then awaiting reclassification (see page 107). Samples of mycelium associated with honey fungus fruitbodies were collected from throughout a 6 hectare woodland in northern Michigan. To the surprise of the researchers all the

FACING PAGE: Pearly Webcap – *Cortinarius alboviolaceus* in a fairy ring

mycelial samples turned out to have an identical genetic blueprint; not only were they all from the same species, the analysis indicated that the samples were all from the same individual. Given the shape of the wood, this meant that at its longest point the mycelium had covered over 5 km, rather more than that in the 800 m diameter fairy ring. Based on the faster growth rates (compared with fairy ring champignon) observed in this species, it was calculated that the mycelium had been growing for at least 1,500 years, making it the oldest known mushroom.

Big is Beautiful

As in many other branches of natural history, mycologists have long been interested in records, including those for the biggest mushroom mycelium and the largest mushroom fruitbody. In the preceding chapters covering fairy rings and the age of mushrooms it has been shown that the record age of an individual mycelium is not from a large fairy ring, but from a species of honey fungus growing in a wood in north America. A different species of honey fungus currently holds the record for the largest mycelium. The individual, found in Washington State, was estimated to cover some 6 km^2. This is possibly the largest area occupied by a single individual of any organism in the world.

As for the record weight, this currently belongs to the oldest individual. Its mycelium has been estimated to weigh in excess of 10,000 kg (10 tonnes), putting it in the same league as many whales. The records of large mycelia are recent phenomena, requiring modern technology, but claims for the biggest or heaviest fruitbody have been around for many years. Not all claims can be substantiated, rather like the very large fish that got away.

Chicken of the woods – *Laetiporus sulphureus*

One 19th century claimant has now been disqualified. The 'Doncaster Monster Sandstone Fungus' discovered in a quarry with a supposed fruitbody covering a diameter in excess of 4.5 m is now believed to have been the mycelial growth of dry rot fungus (*Serpula lacrymans*; see page 103). Many bracket fungi produce large and heavy fruitbodies, often consisting of a collection of overlapping

'brackets'. This was true of a specimen of chicken of the woods, previously known as sulphur polypore (*Laetiporus sulphureus*), found in the New Forest and which tipped the scales at a little over 45 kg.

A much larger specimen of giant bracket (*Rigidiporus ulmarius*) grew on an elm stump outside the Mycology Building at the Royal Botanic Gardens, Kew. In 1998 it had a circumference of nearly 5 m and a weight estimated at over 300 kg. There is no evidence to support the rumour that it was fed growth supplements by the staff at Kew. Prior to falling apart by 2003 it was listed as the world's largest fungal fruitbody in the *Guinness Book of Records*

Giant puffballs (*Calvatia gigantea*) frequently live up to their name and provide good copy for local newspapers. A specimen gathered in Canada in 1987 measured 2.64 m across and weighed 22 kg. British records in excess of 10 kg are not unusual. Had the Canadian puffball been left to mature (it was still immature when collected) it is estimated that the fruitbody would have produced more than 10^{25} spores, that is, 10,000,000,000,000,000,000,000,000 spores! As we are not knee deep in giant puffballs it has to be assumed that the chance of any one spore producing a new mycelium and more puffballs is, unlike the puffball, very, very small.

Giant puffball –
Calvatia gigantea

Mushroom Cultivation

For the better part of human history, our forefathers (and more likely our foremothers) with a fondness for eating mushrooms collected them from the wild. As a result they had to contend with unpredictable supplies brought about by changes in the seasons and the weather, along with habitat destruction.

> *It was inevitable, then, that some entrepreneur would recognise the market value of a steady supply of safe, tasty mushrooms and seize the moment to grow them in captivity.*
>
> (George Hudler, 1998)

In *Down the Garden Path*, published in 1932, Beverley Nichols recounts his attempt at mushroom cultivation:

> *I had a field, and I could do what I liked with it. Bears could be kept in it. Holes could be dug in it ... I wanted to grow mushrooms. I went indoors and looked them up in the Encyclopaedia.*
>
> *The Encyclopaedia said 'see Agaricus'. I saw Agaricus, and was rather pained by the squalid atmosphere in which mushrooms appeared to flourish. There were all sorts of references to fresh horse droppings, stained straw, and decayed top-spit loam. Moreover, when one came to the mushrooms themselves, there was no reference to seeds or cuttings, but only to 'spawn'.*
>
> *Spawn? Spawn sounded very obscene ... I turned to Sutton's catalogue ... So I ordered a lot of Amateur's spawn. I also ordered a cartload of manure and quantities of nitrate of soda and sulphate of ammonia. These were recommended as tonics.*
>
> *I did the planting on June 15th, all over the field .... By August 16th ... not a mushroom had appeared. The field of my neighbour, who had done nothing to deserve it, was white with mushrooms .... One day ... I was walking through the kitchen garden by the marrow bed .... Closer inspection revealed ... hundreds of mushrooms .... My gardener came, with maddening slowness and deliberation, to the scene of action. 'Oh yes', he said. 'When you were putting 'em in the field, I just crumbled up a brick of spawn and shoved it in here for luck' ... 'Rummy things, mushrooms. You can't keep 'em down'.*
>
> *Personally, I now prefer prawns.*

FACING PAGE:
Spawn (mycelium) of cultivated mushroom – *Agaricus bisporus*

Despite the limited success recorded by Mr Nichols, many farmers deliberately introduced mushroom spawn into their meadow land before World War II. Some 70 years later the annual worldwide cultivation of edible mushrooms exceeds 4 million tonnes, of which species of *Agaricus* account for over 40%. Varieties of the so-called cultivated mushroom, *Agaricus bisporus*, provide the bulk of the British mushroom crop, which was worth over £100 million in 2000. There are nearly 600, mostly family-run, mushroom farms in Great Britain.

The history of mushroom cultivation in Europe is obscured by the fact that many early accounts of mushroom sales do not differentiate between the cultivated mushroom (*Agaricus bisporus*), the field mushroom (*Agaricus campestris*) and the horse mushroom (*Agaricus arvensis*); the former grown as a crop, the latter two species collected from the wild. The cultivated mushroom does occur in the wild, but unlike field and horse mushrooms is more likely to be associated with manure or to grow in parkland or at field edges. It differs from other mushrooms in that it produces its spores in pairs rather than in groups of four. The field mushroom does not grow well under cultivation.

The initiators of mushroom cultivation in the West were the French who, realising that mushrooms sometimes arose from areas in gardens (such as melon beds) that had been enriched with stable manure, started to give nature a helping hand. Louis XIV is said to have ordered his chief agronomist, Olivier de Serres, to find a way to grow mushrooms all year round. *Le Jardinière François*, first published in 1650, provides an insight into these early methods:

> *... you must prepare a bed of Mules, or Asses soyl, covering it over four fingers thick with short, and rich dung, and when the great heat of the bed is qualified, you must cast upon it all the parings, and offalls of such Mushrooms as have been dressed in your Kitchen, together with the water wherein they were washed ...*

In 1699 the English diarist John Evelyn wrote about the French practice of preparing hot beds, and in 1707 the eminent botanist Joseph Tournefort pronounced that mushroom 'seeds' must be present in the manure. For British mushroom growers it was the horse that provided the necessary manure. By the early part of the 19th century mushroom production moved inside; Sir Joseph Banks became one of the first people in Britain to own a mushroom house. For the French 'inside' meant growing mushrooms in disused stone quarries (these were more like caves than our notion of quarries) some of which extended under Paris. To this day the cultivated mushroom is known in France as *champignon de Paris*.

Contrary to popular opinion, mushrooms do not need to be grown in the dark, but old underground workings provide cheap accommodation with relatively constant humidity and low-temperature conditions (cool temperatures promote fruiting).

Mushroom growing in the Chislehurst Cave, 1934

Cultivated magic mushrooms are usually dried

Mushrooms are still grown in old limestone workings at Bradford-on-Avon (the practice started there in 1870) and were once produced in a disused railway tunnel in Edinburgh. Some years ago I was contacted by a local radio station and asked to comment about a plan to produce mushrooms in some of Yorkshire's disused coal mines. It was only when I noticed the date, 1st April, that I realised I was having my leg pulled.

It was not until 1893 that a method for obtaining mushroom spawn from germinating the spores ('seeds') was perfected. Before this, spawn gatherers collected mushroom mycelium from areas rich in horse manure. Small amounts of this spawn were inserted into 'bricks' made of a soil and manure mix and the bricks were used to 'seed' mushroom beds (and fields, as described by Mr Nichols at the start of this chapter). At about the same time a system of growing mushrooms on shelves was initiated in America.

By the early 20th century most cultivated mushrooms were a creamy-brown colour, with darker scales on the cap surface. By then spawn was being produced from tissue taken from mushroom fruitbodies and grown on culture media under sterile conditions. This method is the equivalent of taking plant cuttings and, unlike using spore-produced spawn, ensures that the size, texture and taste of the mushrooms are exactly the same as those from which the tissue was taken. In 1927 a small group of smooth, white-capped fruitbodies was detected in a bed of brown mushrooms (possibly the result of a mutation) and these became the basis for the white-capped strain that is the most widely available today.

One major change for modern mushroom growers is the shortage of horse manure, and mushroom compost is now made from a mix of horse manure, poultry litter (providing nitrogen) and straw (providing carbon). Other ingredients commonly used include ground corn cobs and cocoa shells. Powdered urea is sometimes added and gypsum provides both nutrients and the optimum acidity of pH 6.6. The compost heats up to between 58 and 60°C, and the heat initiates chemical and physical changes essential for good mushroom growth. A final 12 hours at around 70°C acts as a pasteurisation and helps to reduce contamination of the crop by bacteria, viruses, insect pests and other fungi. Spawn is added and the temperature kept at about 25°C for 14 days before the casing is added. The casing (a layer spread on top of the compost) is now mostly peat based, made less acidic with the addition of ground limestone. At this stage the temperature is reduced to about 15°C. The stress of this lower temperature initiates the development of fruitbodies. These form in the casing, resulting in a much cleaner crop.

In 1990 David Pegler noted: 'In Britain, apart from a few exotic species in specialised shops, only the Cultivated Mushroom (*Agaricus bisporus*) is usually sold'. For 60 years the white mushroom reigned supreme, but times have changed; white is no longer the only colour. The farm in Bradford-on-Avon now produces button mushrooms that are a strain of the original brown-capped (chestnut) mushroom, sold under the name Crimini. These are produced organically (without the use of inorganic additions to the compost or chemical pesticides). Open brown caps are marketed as Portobellas. As with brown bread, it is all about taste, health and snob value. Since the 1990s the pavement mushroom (*Agaricus bitorquis*) has joined its relative as a commercially grown species. It fruits at a higher temperature and is more suited to summer production. As we shall see in the next chapter, *Agaricus* is no longer the only group of mushrooms available in the shops; the exotics have risen up in a quiet revolution.

Cultivating and Collecting Exotics

In 1992 Peter Blackburne-Maze wrote an article on mushrooms for *The Garden*, in which he stated:

> *Unlike other nationalities, though, we British are terribly conservative, even timid, about what we eat and never more so than when confronted with what looks like a toadstool. Three specialist growers, however, are now concentrating on 'weirdies' and … some pretty unusual foods, especially among the fungi, are now sold in our more adventurous stores.*

Fifteen years on and most supermarkets and many local outlets are selling an ever-expanding range of exotic mushrooms, a high percentage of which are collected from the wild or cultivated here in Britain. This change in the nation's shopping habits has gone hand in hand with a proliferation of restaurant dishes offering such delights as 'wild mushroom risotto' or 'pasta with porcini'.

Unlike the ubiquitous *Agaricus bisporus* (cultivated mushroom) which grows on compost, most of the cultivated exotics grow on dead wood. Some of these have a long history of cultivation in the Far East, but the introduction of new technology has facilitated a move by British growers into producing fresh supplies for supermarkets, farmers' markets and restaurateurs. Several specialist firms supply bags of growing medium and the starter spawn to small-scale producers.

Among the first of the exotics to be cultivated in Britain was the oyster mushroom (*Pleurotus ostreatus*), a species (like the cultivated mushroom) that is native to Britain and on most mushroom hunters' wish list. At least it has gills and is mushroom-like, although the more conservative consumer has to come to terms with a mushroom that has its stem to the side rather than in the middle. Oyster mushrooms grow on living, fallen and dead wood and even on coniferous wood. They can be cultivated in gardens on logs, the spawn being introduced on 'plugs' into predrilled holes or, more intensively, indoors, on bags of sawdust, straw and even coffee waste. Unlike many of the other exotics, the cultivation of oyster mushrooms came to us from North America rather than the Far East.

FACING PAGE:
Oyster mushroom – *Pleurotus ostreatus*

Many outlets now sell a rainbow mix of oyster mushrooms consisting of the blue–grey native species, the yellow-coloured *Pleurotus citrinopileatus*, native to the Far East, and a rosy-pink form of the tropical *Pleurotus djamor*. For the real connoisseur there are kits available for production of the chocolate cap oyster mushroom and even the Yorkshire oyster mushroom, the latter a particularly fine strain of our common native species collected 'from an ancient woodland in Yorkshire' – I know the log from where it came! The tarragon oyster mushroom (sold as *Pleurotus euosmus*, but probably a form of *ostreatus*) lives up to its name for those who want a mushroom with an unusual taste.

The exotic fungus that has really taken off in the new millennium is shiitake, also known as the oak mushroom, black forest mushroom and the king of mushrooms. *Lentinula edodes*, to give it its scientific name, is native to the Far East, where it grows on the dead wood of oaks and chestnuts. In parts of China and Japan it has been cultivated for over 1,000 years. Traditionally, this involved introducing the mycelium into sawn oak logs, but this method necessitated the felling of thousands of trees and had a lead-in time of 18 months before the first crop of fruitbodies. The introduction of techniques involving bagged oak sawdust reduced the lead-in time to less than 8 weeks and encouraged British growers to start producing them.

The chunky brown shiitake is mushroom shaped and has a wonderful, almost smoky flavour and a very firm, meaty texture. In parts of rural Wales it is being produced, on a small scale, to supply local retailers and organic box schemes. It is also made into a wonderful pâté and a medicinal extract (see page 176). For those unable to obtain fresh supplies, shiitake dries well, which intensifies its flavour.

Shiitake is not native to Britain, but another Eastern delicacy is. Velvet shank or winter mushroom (*Flammulina velutipes*) grows on the dead or dying wood of a wide range of deciduous trees and shrubs where, unusually, its clusters of brown fruitbodies are most prolific from late October through to March. Its brown velvety stems are too tough to eat and the caps are lacking in flavour, but not many species fruit through the winter. Cultivated in the Far East for at least 1,200 years as enoki or enokitake (meaning snow peak mushroom), the cultivated product bears little relationship to the wild velvet shank. Enokitake is produced in bottles to which collars are attached. Under very low light conditions this results in pale clusters of long, thin, white stalks, topped with tiny white caps. Fresh enokitake makes a superb addition to stir fries, soups and rice-based dishes.

Lion's mane (monkey head or pom-pom fungus) is about as far removed from a button mushroom as one could imagine. When fresh, it is roughly spherical and covered with white, stalactite-like projections. When dry it is reminiscent of a bathroom sponge. Known in Britain as bearded tooth (*Hericium erinaceus*), it is one of our few native fungi to be protected under the Wildlife and Countryside Act of 1981. It is very rare in the wild, with most records associating it with ancient beech trees. It is, however, relatively easy to cultivate, using production techniques similar to those for growing oyster mushrooms.

Paddy straw mushroom (*Volvariella volvacea*), another species cultivated in Asia (traditionally outdoors on rice-straw), can also be grown on a variety of materials of plant origin. It has been slower to catch on as a fresh crop in Britain, partly because of its rather glutinous texture, but also as it has a basal cup (volva) to the stem. Mushroom hunters are very wary of species emerging from a volva, as these include death cap and related species of *Amanita* (see page 129). This warm-loving species is beginning to turn up as an alien on woodchip (see page 59) in southern England, so may yet find its way into the hearts and stomachs of wild mushroom hunters in Britain.

Three edible bracket fungi are now available as spawn for mushroom growers. These are chicken of the woods (*Laetiporus sulphureus*), hen of the woods (*Grifola frondosa*) and dryad's saddle (*Polyporus squamosus*). I love to grill the chicken-breast-textured *Laetiporus*, but some people are allergic to it, so beware. *Grifola* (collected from the base of oak trees) was sometimes sold in Victorian markets and is better known today as the Japanese maitake, said to contain cancer-preventing chemicals.

Two other native edible species are now being cultivated on compost in a manner similar to the cultivated mushroom. These are field blewit or blue leg (*Lepista saeva*) and wood blewit (*Lepista nuda*), known in French as pied bleu, the name under which they are usually sold. Wood blewits collected from the wild have long been sold in markets around the Sheffield area and are not uncommon in gardens; I enjoyed a fine crop from a rotting heap of beech leaf mould in 2007. They are also taking to woodchip.

Cultivation of a different kind has recently come to Britain in the form of the summer truffle (*Tuber aestivum*) (see page 87). This is one of a number of wild edible species that forms ectomycorrhizal associations with living trees (see page 53) and can only be 'cultivated' on the roots of inoculated trees. Other mushrooms with a high value that are mycorrhizal include cep and other species of *Boletus*, chanterelle (*Cantharellus cibarius*),

Collecting ceps and chanterelles

horn of plenty (*Craterellus cornucopoides*) and wood hedgehog (*Hydnum repandum*), the latter known commercially as champignons mouton. The worldwide consumption of ceps and chanterelles is in excess of 200,000 tonnes a year.

The above-mentioned species cannot be cultivated indoors, so the huge increase in demand for them, especially from British restaurateurs, but also from abroad, has spawned a new breed of mushroom hunters, the professional collectors. By the end of the last millennium over 350 people were collecting 'mushrooms' with a value of some £400,000 a year, and this was only in Scotland. Many others are collecting in Wales and more controversially in the New Forest, where the Forestry Commission introduced a code for amateur collectors and took the owner of a business based on commercial collecting to court. The total trade in UK wild mushrooms is now worth over £3 million a year.

Much of this collecting is done without the landowner's permission and is the cause for resentment in some areas of Britain. So far we have not seen scenes like those in France where there have been reports of townies (*les urbains*) travelling up to 150 km to gather mushrooms without rural landowners' permission. Pensioners in their eighties have had their baskets of mushrooms stolen and car tyres have been slashed. Hopefully, mushroom wars will not break out on this side of the Channel.

Truffles

In November 2004 a white (Piedmont) truffle (*Tuber magnatum*) was sold in London at a charity auction. At 850 g, it was the size of a large potato and, although not the biggest ever found, it attracted huge media attention when it was knocked down for £28,000. The owner of Zafferano, an Italian restaurant in Knightsbridge who acquired the ultimate object of culinary desire, had the misfortune of discovering that his truffle had gone off in the refrigerator while he awaited the return of his head chef from holiday.

Prices of any objects at charity auctions are frequently considerably higher than on the open market, but the white truffle is, weight for weight, one of the most expensive foods in the world. By 2007 the average price had tripled since the start of the millennium to around £5,000 per kilogram, reflecting a similar large rise in the price of gold over the same period. By the time diners receive their truffle shavings, given the usual mark-up, it might be cheaper for them to eat the same weight of 24-carat gold. In 2007 a New York restaurant offered a $25,000 dessert which combined shavings of gold and truffle with top-quality chocolate and cream. It has since been declared the most expensive dessert in the world. To the uninitiated, no food can be worth that much.

As with any commodity, price is related to supply and demand. For the two most desired species of truffle, the white Piedmont (*Tuber magnatum*) and the black Perigord (*Tuber melanosporum*), supply has gone down at a time when demand has increased; hence the price hike. What is it that makes the underground fruitbodies of certain fungi so desirable? The answer lies in a combination of aroma and taste. One uninitiated journalist described the smell of a white truffle as having undertones of diesel and farmyard slurry but, as with wine buffs, those who are hooked use a different vocabulary.

In his very readable book about truffles, Jean-Marie Rocchia waxes lyrically about his responses to eating scrambled eggs with shavings of his native black Perigord truffle:

> *You can fall into an ecstatic trance, become intoxicated, rapturous, gorge yourself, be bewitched, drugged and utterly addicted to the perfume of the truffle for days on end, yet the range of its taste sensations can be totally experienced in a few mouthfuls .... It is a*

FACING PAGE: Gathering truffles, from 'Tacuinum Sanitatis' (15th century)

reassuring perfume, a soothing one which leaves behind an impression of peace and well-being .... It is a perfume which evokes a mother's bosom .... To summarise, the truffle is a vegetable whose perfume has something animal about it.

The last statement is more than poetic licence as scientists have discovered that truffles contain alpha-androsterol, a compound that is found in the saliva (and hence the breath) of rutting boars. This works as a pheromone, and along with other chemicals appears to decrease sexual inhibitions in sows. There is no proof that the chemical has the same effect on women, but the lure of truffles has long been intensified by their supposed aphrodisiacal properties. In truth this is more likely to be because many truffles are comparable in shape and surface texture to human testicles, but the sexual mystique does wonders for the price of truffles.

A white truffle weighing 1.5 kg which sold at auction in 2007 for $330,000

The two most highly prized species of edible truffle mentioned above are native to mainland Europe (particularly between 40 and 47 °N latitude) and are not found wild in Britain. The white truffle grows in central and northern Italy and to a limited amount in neighbouring Slovenia and nearby Croatia. Smooth-skinned, it is reminiscent of a slightly yellow potato or iris rhizome and has an aroma of cheesy garlic. The fungus forms mycorrhizal associations with trees (see page 53) including species of poplar, willow and oak. The collecting season is relatively short (another reason for the high price), typically from October to December. To date, despite attempts over many decades, no one in Italy or elsewhere has succeeded in farming white truffles from trees inoculated with either the fungal spores or mycelial threads.

The black truffle is more cosmopolitan in its distribution and is found in open scrub or woodland on well-drained calcareous hillsides in southern France, Portugal, Spain and Serbia. Italy, Slovenia and Croatia are blessed with both black and white truffles. Despite its name, the French region of Provence yields far more black diamonds (as the truffles are known on account of their multifaceted, warty black skin) than does Perigord. The trees associated with the black truffle include various species of *Quercus*: pubescent oak, holm oak and kermes oak, plus lime, hazel and even some pines. The longer collecting season runs from the first to the last frosts, from about mid-November to early March. As with wine, the harvest is greatly affected by the weather and so the price fluctuates, but prices in excess of £300 per kilogram have been the norm in recent years.

Finding truffles is no easy matter as the fruitbodies develop underground and only rarely protrude above the soil surface. Fortunately, the truffle aroma not only attracts culinary bouquets, but also is an olfactory beacon for a range of mammals that dig up the fruitbodies to consume them. These include deer, mice, squirrels and wild boar. This is far from disaster for the fungus as the spores are deposited in the faeces of the animal, often over long distances. Sadly, the human nose is rarely able to detect a ripe truffle when it is well buried, so truffle hunters make use of those animals that can.

In parts of France the animal of choice is the pig, the sow to be precise, as she is excited by the smell akin to that produced by a randy boar. Not all pigs have the inclination to seek out truffles and they have a habit of eating their finds; they are also not the easiest of animals to transport in the back of a car. In both France and other countries the animal of choice is usually a dog, with a wide range of breeds being used including alsatians, poodles, labradors and dachshunds. Unlike sows, dogs of either sex are not naturally interested in digging for truffles, but they can be trained. A good truffle hound can fetch over £2,000, so most hunters train their own despite the conundrum that to train a dog needs fresh truffles and to find fresh truffles needs a trained dog!

Various attempts at marketing an electronic truffle detector have proved expensive failures, but truffles can be detected by another method, one that involves flies. The truffle fly (species of midge-like *Suilla*) hovers in swarms above hidden truffles and these swarms are searched for in a laidback fashion by truffle hunters. Female flies burrow into the soil and lay their eggs in the truffles, which are later consumed by the developing grubs: not good news for the vegetarian gastronome.

One reason that the black truffle is much cheaper than its white counterpart is that the former can be farmed. As early as 1811 a French farmer by the name of Joseph Talon found that if he transplanted oak seedlings that had originated from the rooting zones of trees that produced truffles, eventually the young trees also produced truffles. When

Talon's secret leaked out it was copied in many other parts of France and by 1900 around 1,000 tonnes of the truffles were being harvested there every year. The value of this is hinted at in an old Perigord saying:

Your wife, your truffles and your garden must all be carefully guarded from your neighbour.

Truffle plantations (*trufflères*) have to be carefully managed so that sufficient sun heats the soil, which may require aeration in spring and watering in July. Two wars, habitat destruction, soil acidification and a flight from the countryside resulted in the steady decline of French black truffle production to a figure of less than 100 tonnes by the end of the 20th century.

In the 1990s new methods of inoculating trees with the black truffle fungus under more sterile conditions, together with a rise in prices, initiated attempts to grow black truffles outside Europe. New Zealand saw its first truffle harvest in 1993, followed shortly afterwards by Tasmania and later by Texas.

The situation in Britain is that truffle hunting had a long history which only died out just before World War II and is now on the verge of a comeback. There are at least 70 species of fungi in Britain that produce underground fruitbodies, but only a small number of these are edible and worth eating. The best of these is the summer truffle (*Tuber aestivum*). This species is found across much of Europe and is collected and sold (often tinned) in Italy and France, where it is viewed as a poor relative of the similar-looking Perigord truffle, in terms of both its texture and its much less pungent aroma. Writing in 1992, the French author Jean-Marie Rocchia notes that it is found in southern England, 'where it is supremely disdained by the subjects of Her Gracious Majesty'.

British subjects were always a little slow to catch on where mushrooms and toadstools were concerned, despite knowledge from classical times; Pliny described truffles as 'callosities of earth ... distinguished by their colour, which is red, or black, or white within'. The British herbalist Gerard, writing in 1597, included *Tuber terrae* in his famous work, but his description and picture are of a *Cyclamen* corm. By the 17th century we were importing truffles from France, and by the following century the commercial hunting of truffles in southern England (mainly Hampshire, Wiltshire, Sussex and Kent) had begun.

Gilbert White, the renowned naturalist from Selbourne (Hampshire), writing in October 1789, recorded:

A trufle-hunter called on us, having in his pocket several large trufles found in the neighbourhood ... Half a crown a pound was the price, which he asked for this commodity.

At over 25 pence per kilogram this was good money at the time. One-hundred and fifty years later, when the last professional truffle hunter, Alfred Collins, finally retired along with his truffle terriers, the price was only 50 pence per kilogram; today the price is nearer £50 per kilogram and this is one reason for a revival of the ancient art of truffle hunting. In 2004 a farming couple found 10 kilograms of summer truffle near the Wiltshire/Berkshire border. The influence of climate change, with its milder winters, wetter springs and hotter summers, may be to the benefit of British truffles. The very wet summer of 2007 resulted in many more finds of British truffles. Marion Dean, who hails from the same county as Gilbert White, has recently begun to offer training courses for potential truffle dogs, as the English truffle dog appears to have died out as a separate breed. Marion owns a lagotto romagnolo, a breed specifically bred in Italy for truffle hunting.

Sliced black truffle

In 1999 the first British *trufflère*, for the production of black truffles, was planted in a Hertfordshire kitchen garden and 'truffle trees' are now regularly advertised in gardening magazines. As it takes at least 10 years before the fruits of one's labour can be harvested, mycologists and restaurateurs are holding their breath. If, as seems possible, the climate in parts of Italy and France becomes too hot and dry, it may be that Britain will not only take over as a major wine producer but also becomes an exporter of truffles.

The high prices fetched by truffles have resulted in some rather underhand tactics. Just as heroin can be cut with inert substances to increase the profit for the dealer, so summer truffle has been passed off as the more expensive Perigord species. In recent years cheaper black truffle species from China have also been substituted for European truffles. The marbled black interior colour of some truffles is not dissimilar to that of a young earthball (*Scleroderma*), which not only has no market value but is mildly poisonous. Despite this it has been used to bulk up the weight of truffles, one reason why most dealers only purchase whole specimens. In 2007 an Italian collector was the victim of a ram-raiding attack when his portable refrigerator containing £1,400 worth of white truffles was stolen.

Given the increased sophistication of the British palette the demand for truffles is likely to remain high, although the price will be out of reach for many. One solution is to purchase some artificial truffle oil, at about £5 for 250 ml. This can be sprayed on food to give a truffle-like flavour, but is much derided by true connoisseurs of good taste. At least the less affluent can still enjoy truffles: cherry-sized balls of soft chocolate paste enclosed in a dusting of cocoa. These have the appearance of freshly dug truffles, hence the name for the chocolate confectionery.

Of Ballerinas and Ancient Oaks

In 1996, my book *How to Identify Edible Mushrooms* became embroiled in a debate about the possible harm caused by mushroom gatherers. Several commentators attempted to make a link between the decrease in sightings of previously common edible species, including both field and horse mushrooms, and the rise in popularity of collecting mushrooms for culinary purposes as encouraged by books such as mine. I pointed out that over the same time-scale there had also been a more carefully documented decrease in the numbers of many species of British butterfly, but this could hardly be blamed on the eating habits of *Homo sapiens*.

The late Maurice Rotheroe served as conservation officer with the British Mycological Society from 1996 to 2001. He too found himself defending mushroom hunters at a time when the fashion among conservationists was turning against them. Maurice considered that his role was much more about providing good publicity for fungi than engaging in expert taxonomy. In response to the row about mushroom collecting he wrote in *British Wildlife*:

> *The debate over collecting wild mushrooms for the pot appears to have been hijacked by those who use anecdotal and emotive language and ignore the scientific evidence.*

The scientific evidence shows that, contrary to popular belief, there is no proof that the collection of fruitbodies creates a threat to the species concerned. One such study showed no decline in fruitbody numbers over a 13 year period. In the short term, the removal of older fruitbodies actually stimulates the growth of replacement fruitbodies in much the same way that gardeners remove old flowers to encourage new ones. Research has shown that, as with all other wildlife, the most serious threat to mushrooms and toadstools comes from habitat loss. Fungi, along with many plants and animals, have suffered from the loss of ancient woodlands and a reduction in the hectarage of unimproved, grazed grassland. For those fungi that are restricted to one plant species, fungal frequency is directly linked to host numbers.

In 1995 Maurice Rotheroe neatly encapsulated the problem of host specificity, along

The ballerina – *Hygrocybe calyptriformis*

with some of the other issues involved with the recording and protection of rare species of fungus. He wrote about the U-turn executed by the Crown Estate in rescinding its decision to tidy up parts of Windsor Great Park by felling some 20 ancient oak trees. It had been pointed out to them that one of the old trees was host to 25% of the known British population of the robust bracket (*Phellinus robustus*). This fungus produces a woody, lopsided bracket, the yellow to rust-brown undersurface of which is covered in minute pores. It is a parasite on oak and typically produces its brackets high up on the trunk or on thicker side branches of very old (veteran) trees.

Maurice recorded:

The reasons for its rarity are becoming more obvious. To begin with, 275-year old oak trees are rare. Secondly, mycologists are rare. Rarer still are mycologists who can spot a bracket fungus 20 feet up a tree. Rarest of all are mycologists who are still young and fit enough to climb an oak tree to identify the fungus.

If a fungus gains a rarity value in part because it is hard to spot and difficult to identify, it may also develop a low profile if it fruits only rarely. We can be pretty certain that the dodo is extinct as there have been no recent sightings of this enigmatic bird, but lack of recent sightings of a bracket or an agaric fungus does not preclude its presence hidden in a tree or in the soil. If there are not enough mycologists recording the species throughout the British Isles, the few records we have may not reflect its true frequency. Entomologists and botanists have produced detailed maps depicting the frequency and distribution of butterflies and plants across Britain, from which we can elucidate not only which are the rare species, but also those showing a rapid decline in numbers and thus most in need of protection. This has resulted in species being placed on Red Data Lists and has provided a framework for conservation.

Until very recently there were few such comprehensive records for mushrooms owing to a lack of both mycologists and money. Following the signing of the international Convention of Biological Diversity in 1992, the conservation of endangered species was considered under Biodiversity Action Plans (BAPs). For those fungi given a BAP, funding was provided to encourage forays in likely habitats in an attempt to determine just how restricted the species was. One species covered under a BAP was pink waxcap (*Hygrocyybe calyptriformis*) or the ballerina, to give it one of its more delightful older names. There are about 50 species of waxcap, mostly confined to unimproved grassland, but including a number of quite common, if not all easily identifiable species. In contrast, pink waxcap is readily recognisable, but had been recorded from fewer than 50 sites in Britain by the early 1990s.

Backed by pictures of the fungus, the charity Plantlife asked its members to look for the pink waxcap and send in records during 2002 and 2003. The result was astounding: 200 new sites. At the time I was teaching a course in a large Victorian house in Chesterfield. During the coffee break I took the class onto the lawn and there were two fruitbodies of pink waxcap in a very urban setting. This exercise showed the problems involved in regarding a species as endangered simply because it had not been recorded in very many places.

The raised awareness given to species with a BAP also served to encourage mycologists to seek for supposedly rare species. For my own part I had never seen one of these, the oak polypore *Piptoporus quercinus*, a bracket which, like the robust bracket championed by Maurice Rotheroe, is restricted to ancient oak trees. In the summer of 2005 I visited Calke Park, famous for its ancient oaks (many more than 400 years old) and within 30 minutes was delighted to find oak polypore. Calke was one of just 18 known sites and its picture (upside down) featured in the National Trust's guide to the Park. Having seen it once, I am now on the lookout for new sites.

The *Red Data List of Threatened British Fungi* was published in 2007. Only two of some 27 BAP species are still considered to be endangered, largely as a result of survey work such as that outlined above and the growth of local mycology groups. Those that are on the threatened list include sand-dune and native pinewood species, both limited habitats that have been well recorded, along with rare species associated with mature beechwoods.

Seventy-six species are listed as extinct, although in the past this category has proved a difficult one. In late 1999 a retired forester was walking in Kielder Forest when he saw what looked like a willow stem covered in red paint. It turned out to be a scarlet patch-forming fungus (*Cytidia calicina*), a species last recorded in 1900 and long thought to be extinct in Britain. It has since been spotted in Scotland. The chances of an amateur mushroom hunter finding a species that is new to Britain (see page 29), or one thought to be threatened or even extinct, are surprisingly high; the main problem is realising that the find is unusual and getting the record verified.

A Code of Conduct for Mushroom Hunters

With a growing interest in mycology has come the need for a set of ground rules. There is no evidence that careful removal of fruitbodies has a detrimental effect, but too much trampling can result in the death of underlying mushroom mycelium. Fungal fruitbodies provide food for animals and the larval stages of insects. Woody material moved in the search for fungi should be replaced. The key points are:

The countryside is a working landscape.

Follow the Countryside and Access codes.

Respect the natural environment.

Wildlife needs mushrooms too, so only pick what you will use.

Take care not to damage or over-trample the vegetative part of a mushroom.

Do not collect unexpanded mushrooms as these will not have released any spores.

Only remove dead wood if it is needed as an aid to identification.

Use a field guide, eliminating collection of unwanted species.

Pick no more than 1.5 kg and no more than half of the fruitbodies of any single species.

It is good manners to ask the landowner's permission before collecting mushrooms.

Be aware that collecting may be banned or restricted on nature reserves or land owned by bodies such as the National Trust and Forestry Commission (especially in parts of the New Forest).

Help is also at hand for landowners in the form of a leaflet entitled *Managing Your Land with Fungi in Mind*, produced by the Fungus Conservation Forum in 2001.

Fungi that Glow in the Dark

In 21st century Britain, urban sprawl and its resultant light pollution from street and security lights is a source of great irritation to amateur astronomers as it decreases their chance of seeing the dim glow of some of our more distant stars. Mycologists and others are also denied the pleasure of experiencing the glow of more earthly bodies; the light produced by fungi. Pliny, writing in the 1st century AD, describes a luminous fungus:

> *this fungus grows on the top of the tree and gives out a brilliant light at night; this indeed is the sign by which its presence is known, and by the aid of this light it may be gathered at night.*

Allowing for a little artistic licence, the passage almost certainly refers to *Omphalotus olearius*, an orange agaric, looking like a large chanterelle, that grows at the base of olive trees in Mediterranean regions. The status of this fungus in Britain is in doubt. There are rare records of a very similar species, *Omphalotus illudens*, which grows on sweet chestnut in southern England. This is more frequent in parts of the United States, where its ability to glow in the dark has given rise to its common name of jack o'lantern. Recent work indicates that British *Omphalotus* specimens may in fact belong to the same species as that described by Pliny.

Despite Pliny's early observation of a light-emitting fungus, the link between fungi and the luminosity of rotting wood and leaf litter was not made in Britain until the 19th century. Before this the faint glow associated with woodland areas was variously described as foxfire and faerie light. The pale blue–green light typical of fungal luminescence gave rise to countless stories of ghosts, will o' the wisps and fairies. The great 8th century tale of Beowulf includes a possible reference to fungal luminescence:

> *... the lake stands shadowed by trees stiff with hoar-frost. A wood, firmly rooted, frowns over the water. There, night after night, a fearful wonder may be seen – fire on the water ...*

Ben Jonson, in the 17th century, made a guess as to the cause of the light emitted from rotting wood:

> *While she sits reading by the glow-worms light*
> *Or rotten wood o'er which the worm hath crept.*

FACING PAGE: Bioluminescent fruitbody of *Mycena cyanophus*

Mark Twain was rather more accurate in his observations in *The Adventures of Huckleberry Finn*, where he mentions:

> *Rotten chunks that's called 'Foxfire' that just makes a soft kind of glow when you lay them in a dark place.*

In Britain the name touchwood was given to the rotten wood and there are accounts of children enjoying the thrill of reading under the bedclothes by the light provided by glowing wood. There are numerous more practical stories involving the use of luminous wood. Various 17th century reports from northern Europe indicate that the wood was used to mark paths through forests and as a form of safety lamp where a naked flame would be dangerous. The lack of light experienced by soldiers moving around trenches in World War I was apparently solved by some soldiers who fixed bits of rotten wood to their helmets. In World War II there were reports of the glowing wood from timber yards being covered for fear they might attract enemy bombs.

The most frequent reports of luminous rotten wood in Britain are associated with honey fungus (*Armillaria mellea*), the scourge of foresters and gardeners (see page 108). It was from the mycelial strands of this species that Heller attributed the fungal cause of the luminescence of rotting wood in 1843, although the species responsible was not correctly named until 30 years later. The light is strongest from freshly broken rotting wood. Other British wood-rotting fungi that glow in the dark include the well-known sulphur tuft (*Hypholoma fasciculare*), the edible velvet shank (*Flammulina velutipes*) and the diminutive candlesnuff fungus (*Xlaria hypoxylon*). Of those that produce a glow from leaf litter many, such as lilac bonnet, are species of *Mycena*. The Victorian mycologist Worthington Smith once observed both the mycelium and fruitbody of root fomes (*Heterobasidion annosum*) glowing in a mine in Wales.

The light emitted by fungal mycelia is continuous (although it is not visible during daylight) and is produced without heat. As with a similar light emitted by some species of mollusc, it is known that the fungal light results when a chemical called luciferin, rich in phosphorus, combines with oxygen in the presence of an enzyme. Some commentators have sought a reason for the light, including attracting night-flying insects that might subsequently spread the spores (unlikely as most fungal luminescence comes from the mycelium, not the fruitbody), but it is probably an unusual by-product of fungal metabolism.

FACING PAGE:
Sulphur tuft – *Hypholoma fasciculare*

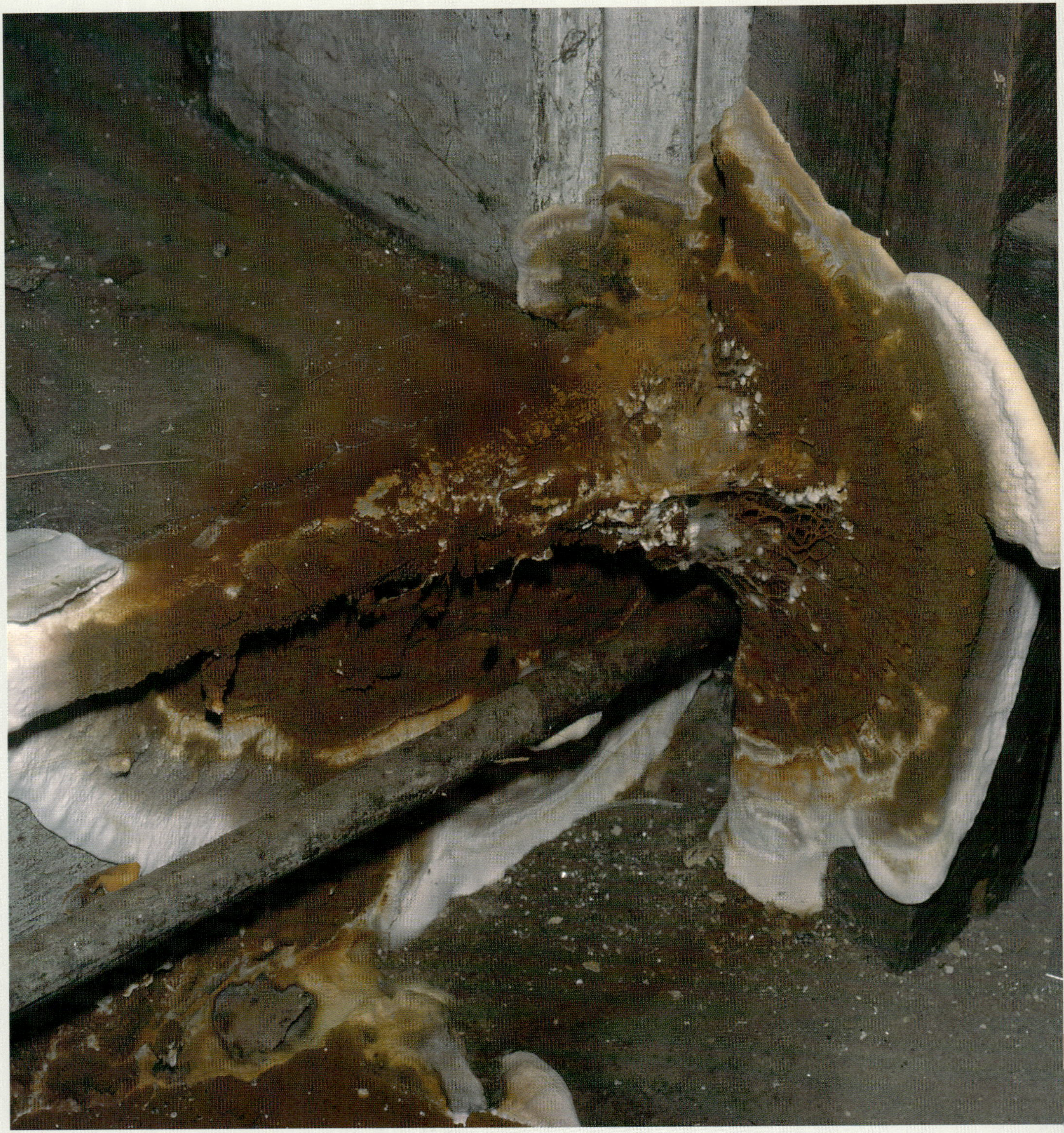

A Plague Upon your House

The Old Testament book of Leviticus, chapter 14, verse 35, says:

And he that owneth the house shall come and tell the priest, saying
It seemeth to me there is, as it were, a plague in the house.

The subsequent verses give more details of the 'plague', including its presence in the walls of the house. There is mention of a greenish or reddish colour under the house walls and the need to remove any dust from the house to a site away from the city. Whatever the cause of the ancient problem in the Middle East, this Biblical reference will resonate with anyone who has discovered that their property has been infected by dry rot.

The very name dry rot is close to being an oxymoron, as rot is always associated with dampness. Ben Jonson declared:

It is a misnomer to call it dry rot for the trouble is invariably due to dampness.

The name is, however, an apt description of the state of any timber after it has been infected: dry, brittle and powdery. The scientific name, *Serpula lacrymans*, provides more information. *Serpula* comes from the Latin for a little serpent, which is a fanciful description of the sinuous wrinkles of the orange–brown, pancake-like fruitbodies of the fungus. The specific *lacrymans* is a derivative of the Latin word for a tear, referring to the drops of water produced on the fruitbodies and timber surfaces in the early stages of infection. A Victorian mycologist waxed lyrically about the teardrops as if the fungus was 'weeping in regret for the havoc it has made'. In the 21st century the tears are more likely to be those of a householder facing a large bill to remedy the problem.

Previous scientific names include *Merulius lacrymans* (see page 106) and *Boletus lacrymans*. Boletus is the scientific name for woodland fungi known as the boletes which include cep, one of the most prized of all edible mushrooms. These have tubes in place of the gills typical of most agarics. Although dry rot is an ally of the bracket fungi (albeit with a much softer fruitbody) it is even more closely related to the boletes as its spores are produced from short tubes embedded in the fruitbody.

FACING PAGE: Dry rot – *Serpula lacrymans*, showing the fruitbody

Dry rot is less common than it was in former times. It only appears as an 'alien' in the recent checklist of British Basidiomycota for the simple reason that it has never been recorded in this country other than in artificial habitats; it is confined to structural timber, particularly that used in buildings and boats. It occurs as a wild, wood-rotting fungus in the forests of North America, Central Europe and the Himalayas where it rots conifers. Softwoods such as pine and spruce are most prone to attack when used as structural timber.

Despite its name, primary infection by dry rot requires wood with a moisture content of more than 20% plus conditions of high humidity and a temperature in the range of 0–28°C. Initial growth of the fungus gives rise to dense sheets of mycelium, resembling cotton-wool. Later, thick, tough, hyphal strands are formed that are able to pass through minute holes in cement, plaster, mortar, bricks and stone. The strands can extend for several metres (the record is 8 metres) and may run under floorboards and along water pipes, telephone wires and electric cables. In this way dry timber and other nutrient resources including clothes, leather shoes and even books come within reach of the spreading fungus, even if the necessary water has to be transported from the original infection site. Cellulose in wood is decomposed, leaving behind a dry, brown, brittle matrix of lignin. Infected wood loses its structural strength, resulting in people falling through floors and stairways, and even in roof collapse where rafters are infested.

The pancake-like fruitbodies may extend to cover several square metres and produce enormous numbers of brown spores. The daily production of spores released from a medium-sized fruitbody can be as great as 20 million. A cocoa-like deposit spilling out from behind a skirting board (resembling the Biblical dust?) is often the first sign of any problem, along with a faint smell of mushrooms. Fruitbodies can develop on any solid surface, including objects made of glass or metal. Treatment includes the elimination of any original water source, often the result of a leaking pipe, and improved ventilation to prevent water resulting from condensation. All infected timber has to be replaced with new, protected material, while wood and brickwork in the surrounding area around the infection require treatment with chemicals and heat to prevent reinfection.

The scourge of dry rot in British houses reached a peak in the 20 years following World War II. Bomb damage and neglect were succeeded by the use of cheaper softwoods in the construction industry and the spread of central heating; warmth accelerates fungal growth. The recent flooding of hundreds of homes in low-lying parts of Britain could precipitate a surge in dry-rot infections. Preventive treatment is one reason for the painfully slow reinstatement of flood-affected properties.

Before the introduction of 'ironclads' in 1863, the severity of fungal rot in the Royal Navy's fleet of wooden war ships was more newsworthy than the problem in houses. British oak was the principal timber for ship building. Dry, well seasoned, adequately ventilated oak was rarely infected with dry rot. The use of cheaper, unseasoned, imported timber (often floated down rivers from its source) and poorly ventilated conditions of the lower decks resulted in damage to and loss of ships commensurate with that resulting from enemy action.

The rotten state of the British Navy came to a head in 1810 with the launch of a 110 gun battleship named *Queen Charlotte* in honour of the wife of King George III. The ship was so badly infected with dry rot that she had to be refitted even before she was commissioned. Within 6 years of being built the cost of repairs had exceeded the original build cost. In 1815 the Royal Society of Arts awarded a gold medal to the finder of the best cure for the problem. The winning suggestion was that infected ships be sunk for several months; a rather drastic and short-term remedy.

The introduction of creosote, from coal tar, in 1838 was at least partially effective in the fight against dry rot. More modern chemicals and application methods have helped to reduce the chance of reinfection. As with human disease, the cost and effectiveness of treatment are strongly correlated with early diagnosis. A modern early-warning signal of the usually hidden symptoms of the early stages of dry-rot infestation is provided, not by new technology but by the use of 'rothounds'. Just as truffle-hunters use trained dogs to detect truffles by their aroma, so specially trained dogs are able to sniff out the weaker scent of dry rot. This negates the need to remove plaster or the use of other destructive techniques in the search for evidence of the fungus.

Dry rot has also entered the literary world, where it is a firm favourite within the genre of horror fiction. Edgar Allen Poe's *The Fall of the House of Usher* depicts:

> *Minute fungi overspread the whole exterior, hanging in a fine tangled web from the eaves. … In this there was much that reminded me of the specious totality of old woodwork which has rotted long years in some neglected vault, with no disturbance from the breath of the external air.*

Dry rot features in more modern fiction in the form of Brian Lumley's award-winning short story in his 1993 collection *Fruiting Bodies and Other Fungi*. The villain of the piece is Merulius (an earlier Latin name for dry rot), a mutant strain of fungus that arrives at the coastal village of Easingham by way of tropical lumber deposited on the strand line. It later gains a 'hypha-hold' on the village buildings. When the story-teller revisits Easingham to renew his acquaintance with the sole remaining inhabitant:

> *All that sat there was a monstrous grey mushroom! It was a great fibrous mass, growing out of and welded into mycelial strands to the settee and in its centre an obscene yellow fruiting body ...*
>
> *I backed away ... into what had once been a piece of furniture .... Soft as a sponge, the thing collapsed and sent me sprawling. Dust and (I imagined) dark red spores rose up everywhere.*

In the interest of science and to prevent nightmares I should point out that the temperature of the human body is too high for normal forms of dry rot, although I cannot speak for mutant strains. In addition, even the most block-headed members of the human race are not composed of wood and thus lack the cellulose that is the essential nutrition for the fungus to live.

Not So Sweet As It Sounds

In 1891 Mordecai Cooke wrote of the honey-coloured stump mushroom (as it was then called):

> *No fungus is perhaps more variable in appearance, and it takes a long time to be sure of it under its many phases.*

In 1975 Roy Watling, one of Britain's most eminent mycologists, produced a booklet for foresters, *Mushrooms and Toadstools of Broadleaved Forests*. Chapter 1 started with Armillaria Mellea: Honey Fungus. After a brief description, Roy wrote:

> *This rather variable, and therefore often perplexing fungus, is a parasite and causes a destructive rot of trees. It can travel long distances through the soil.*

Over the past 30 years Professor Watling has helped to unravel something of the enigmatic nature of what should now strictly be called honey fungi; there are believed to be as many as 12 closely related different species, of which five wood-rotting species occur in Britain. Not only do the five species have different morphological features, explaining the variable nature of what was previously thought to be just one species, but the species differ in their parasitic virulence, host preference and geographic spread throughout Britain.

Does this concern anyone outside the academic world of the professional mycologist? Yes, yes, yes! Honey fungus, as it is still widely known, causes a destructive rot of trees resulting in millions of pounds worth of damage every year to foresters and gardeners; the latter have even been known to move house because of it. All five species grow in clusters, usually from stumps or trunk bases, but also from tree roots when they have no obvious above-ground connection with a woody substrate. The honey-brown coloured caps expand to 15 cm across, bearing darker scales at their centres.

In young fruitbodies the gills are covered by a white veil. This later forms a cottony ring on the stem in all but ringless honey fungus (*Armillaria tabescens*). This species

also has pinky-brown mature gills, whereas the others have pale-yellow gills. Honey fungus (*Armillaria mellea*) has a cylindrical stem, while bulbous honey fungus [*Armillaria gallica* (*bulbosa*)] has a yellow-tinted stem with a bulbous base. Dark honey fungus (*Armillaria ostoyae*) has caps of a much darker brown colour. The fifth species, *Armillaria borealis*, is more widespread in Scotland, on birch, ash and spruce. All species of honey fungus produce prodigious amounts of creamy white spores and these often festoon the wood, moss and grass below the caps.

Honey fungus (*Armillaria mellea*) is the most virulent parasite of the four species and is common on a wide range of deciduous trees and shrubs, although less frequent on conifers. Like the other species it can also live on dead wood, from where it may spread to living, undamaged trees by infecting their roots. All four species travel through the soil in the form of bootlace-like strands which can also be found beneath the bark of infected trees. In the past these have been confused with plant roots and tree deaths have been blamed on 'strangling ivy roots'.

Both ringless honey fungus and dark honey fungus are less virulent parasites, the former typically fruiting on oak, beech or hornbeam roots in central and southern England, the latter on both deciduous and coniferous species, especially on acid soils in Scotland. Bulbous honey fungus is only weakly parasitic, which is fortunate as it is probably the most common species in both Scotland and southern England.

Armillaria species have been responsible for many garden tree and shrub deaths, including fruit trees, privet, Leyland cypress, rhododendrons and even monkey puzzle. The tubers of iris and potatoes are also vulnerable. In forestry the root butt rot resulting from honey fungus infection makes trees liable to windthrow (blowing over) and snapping near the base. There is no effective fungicidal control.

Victorian mycologists were not impressed with the culinary properties of honey fungus; one described it as 'a nauseous disagreeable fungus' (the cut flesh has a strong odour). Another deemed it 'tough, bitter, and not at all pleasant', while acknowledging that it was always in demand in Vienna. Honey fungus is now more acceptable and immigrants from Poland and other eastern European countries are among those who collect the unexpanded fruitbodies for pickling. Some people find honey fungus difficult to digest, so it is still not on the edible and excellent list. Nothing about honey fungus is straightforward.

FACING PAGE:
Honey fungus – *Armillaria mellea* note the cylindrical stem, ring and cap scales

Stands the church clock at ten to three
And is there honey fungus still for tea?
Perhaps not.

With apologies to Rupert Brook

There are some good things to say about honey fungus. First, it holds the record for the oldest and biggest fungus (see page 71). Secondly, rotting wood impregnated by its mycelia gives off an eerie glow in the dark (see page 99). Finally, some tropical tree-growing (epiphytic) orchids parasitise honey fungus which has itself parasitised the tree: the orchid gets its nutrients from the tree via the fungal mycelium. At least something sweet has come from honey fungus.

Boring Beetles and the Elm Decline

I have just returned from walking my dog. As the two of us passed a small windbreak I could see that the swelling buds of oak, beech and sycamore were heralding the oncoming spring. Four trees were bereft of buds and bark, their pale dead wood stood starkly against the winter sky. Closer inspection revealed hieroglyphic-like markings etched into the wood surface. The four dead trees represented a tiny fraction of the 25 million British elms that have died as a result of Dutch elm disease since the start of the current epidemic in 1965. By the mid-1980s some 90% of the great elms of England had been killed. I have written 'current epidemic' because elm disease has been with us before. A milder form of the disease struck between the two World Wars and also in the 19th century during the early years of Queen Victoria's reign. It now seems likely that the elm decline (when the amount of elm pollen decreased by over 50% in just a few years) in the early Neolithic period (*c.* 3,800 BC) also resulted from the disease.

Dutch elm disease is caused by a fungus that induces wilting as a result of blockages to the tree's water-conducting vascular system. It is not restricted to the Dutch elm; all species and races of elm tree in Britain are vulnerable, including the ubiquitous wych elm, although the English elm has proved the most susceptible. The Dutch epithet does not indicate the origin of the disease: the name resulted from research carried out in Holland into the European epidemic in the first half of the 20th century. Many species of tree are parasitised by macrofungi that produce bracket-like fruitbodies on trunks and branches. The wind-borne spores usually infect healthy trees through scars left when branches fall off. In contrast, Dutch elm disease is caused by a microfungus that does not produce an external fruitbody and whose spores are distributed by insects.

The Dutch research showed that the fungus responsible for harming elm trees was a member of the Ascomycota, in the same great group of fungi as yeasts, truffles and morels. The specific name of the fungus, *Ceratocystis ulmi*, now known as *Ophiostoma ulmi*, was taken from *Ulmus*, the scientific name for elms. Although many British trees were infected in the earlier epidemic, only 10–20% of elms died, mostly in the south of England, and the epidemic began to subside by the end of the 1930s. When, in the 1960s, a more serious epidemic was initiated it was quickly attributed to a more virulent strain of the same fungus. Later research has shown it to be the result of a related species, *Ophiostoma novo-ulmi*. This is the fungus that has changed the landscape in many parts of southern and eastern England, with the death of millions of mature hedgerow elms.

The origin of the two fungal species is unknown, but as with dry rot (see page 103) they may have spread from natural populations in the Himalayan region. The link between the wilt-causing fungi and the activities of the grubs of wood-boring *Scolytus* beetles has long been suspected. The eminent Victorian horticulturalist and landscaper J.C. Loudon wrote in 1838 of an experiment that attempted to prove that the beetles only fed on rotten elm wood, indicating that the fungal attack pre-dated the arrival of the beetles. The true story is more complex than this.

Fertilised female beetles bore through the bark of recently dead elm trees (trees that may have been killed by the fungus) to the woody tissue below. Here they deposit eggs either side of a 3–5 cm long gallery. If the tree from which the female beetle hatched was infected with the fungus then she may be carrying fungal spores that have hitched a ride. Up to 70 grubs emerge from the eggs and eat through the wood at right angles to the gallery. The result is a series of near parallel channels; markings such as those I observed on the debarked dead elms seen during my dog walk. The fungus also grows by feeding on the wood. The beetle grubs feed on the fungus-rotten wood and also on some of the fungal hyphae which produce sticky spores inside the beetle galleries. The grubs turn into pupae, from which both male and female beetles emerge, picking up fungal spores before they bore out through the bark and fly to nearby healthy elm trees where they bore through the bark to feed. After mating, females go in search of recently dead elms.

So an unholy alliance of beetle and fungus has been responsible for the death of millions of *mature* elms during the past 40 years. Despite this there are still plenty of elms in Britain. The reason for this is that the roots of elms are not killed by the fungus and in all species other than wych elms, new suckers sprout from the roots. This apparent phoenix-like resurrection does not result in new big elms; once the new shoots develop bark they are reinfected via the beetle. Wych elms rarely sucker, but young trees produce seeds within 15 years, often before they are infected. The result is a surprising number of *small* elms in Britain, although their future is uncertain. During the writing of this chapter I learnt of the purchase of 60 Princeton Elms by the Prince of Wales to be planted at his Highgrove estate. The trees are a cultivar of *Ulmus americana* which

FACING PAGE: Hieroglyphic-like markings caused by wood-boring beetle larvae

Dying hedgerow elms

appears to be resistant to the disease and has been imported from North America. Other landowners will no doubt be keen to learn how the trees perform over the coming years.

The knock-on effects of so much dead elm wood in the early years of the current epidemic helped to make the greater spotted woodpecker, which feeds and nests in the dead trees, a much more common bird. Conversely, the white-letter hairstreak, a butterfly associated with mature elms, has shown a dramatic decline. During the 1970s and 1980s many decaying elm logs in southern England became colonised by wrinkled peach (*Rhototus palmatus*), a toadstool with a pinky peach-coloured, wrinkled cap and apricot-coloured gills. This previously rare fungus has now returned to its former status owing to a current paucity of dead wood from mature elm trees. A majority of the more recent records for wrinkled peach are from maple, sycamore, beech and ash wood. By 2003 it had been placed on the European Red List of endangered species (see page 94).

Professor Sir Richard Evans, who was once described as the whirling dervish of the biotechnology sector, has reason to be thankful to *Ophiostoma ulmi*. Near the start of his illustrious career he was looking for a method of making a complicated chemical called dexketoprofen, a substance with a strong anti-inflammatory action. He discovered an enzyme in Dutch elm fungus which could make dexketoprufen. By transferring the fungal genes to a bacterium he was able to make lots of the enzyme from which to make dexketoprofen. This became the first drug produced by biotechnology to be approved for medical use in Europe. At least some good has come from Dutch elm fungus.

A Fungal Flasher

The stinkhorn is a fungus that shocks and amuses, delights and revolts, possibly in equal measures. For a mushroom that some find difficult to stomach it is perhaps apt that it belongs to a group of fungi known as the Gasteromycetes or stomach fungi. This relatively small group of species produces spores inside a sac or stomach-like fruitbody, as exemplified by the near-spherical puffballs.

The fruitbody of *Phallus impudicus* (the stinkhorn's scientific name) starts life as a puffball lookalike, about the size, colour and shape of a hen's egg, partly buried among leaf litter in both broadleaved and coniferous woodland. It is easily distinguished from its puffball relatives by the presence of thick white mycelial cords at its base and a clammy feel resulting from the pale-brown, jelly-like layer just beneath its skin. It is also much heavier than a puffball of similar size.

If the stinkhorn simply ripened its spores within the white sac (as puffballs do), the young fruitbody would not have been given names such as devil's egg and witch's egg. Curiously, the egg 'hatches', usually under the cover of darkness. The outcome is not a fluffy chicken, but a very penis-like structure which rises slowly from its sheath of jelly. The acorn-shaped apex is a dull olive–green colour. This contrasts with the stark white of the hollow, polystyrene-like, cylindrical stem. The bottom of the egg is left encircling the stem base rather like a paper bag.

As the stem grows (and it does so at a rate of up to 10 cm an hour, fast enough to see it moving) it does something most unusual for a fungus: it makes a noise! For those brave enough to lie down on the leaf litter and put an ear to the growing phallus, the sound is identical to that made by Rice Krispies when milk is added. By early morning the erection is complete and the 'member' stands 10–15 cm above ground level. At the same time the apical olive, spore-bearing mass (known as the gleba) undergoes a chemical change. The result of this is a darkening of its colour, a change to a slimy texture and the production of a foul smell, described as akin to bad drains or rotting flesh. The horn (formerly known as Satan's member) now has a stink.

Tennyson wrote of his own experience:

As one that smells a foul-fleshed agaric in the holt,
And deems it carrion of some woodland thing,
Or shrew or weasel, nipt her slender nose
With petulant thumb and finger shrilling 'Hence'.

Beatrix Potter, who produced many wonderful paintings of fungi (see page 187), described it as the 'horrid plant like a white stick with a loose cap which smells exactly like a dead sheep'. Apparently she was unable to find the courage to paint it. Another Victorian lady, Charles Darwin's eldest daughter Etty, is said to have collected and burnt stinkhorns from the garden so that they would not be seen by, and become a corrupting influence for, their servants. Some societies are less easily shocked and the fungus has been used in dried powdered form as an aphrodisiac for both humans and farm animals; a sort of fungal Viagra. It has also been used as a 'herbal' medicine in attempts to treat epilepsy and gout. In eastern Europe the egg stage is sliced and eaten raw in salads, a custom that I have only tried once.

Flies are attracted to the fungus by its powerful smell, and while they may be disappointed by the absence of rotting flesh, they rapidly consume the sticky olive gleba, thus exposing the underlying white, honeycomb region. *Phallus* spores are deposited by the flies in tiny specks of dung, an appropriate method of spore dispersal for such a malodorous fungus. Judging by the ubiquitous nature of stinkhorn in Britain this unusual method of spore dispersal is very effective.

Rotting flesh and tales of the unexpected are never far removed from stinkhorns even in our modern society. Towards the end of the 20th century the residents of a small Sussex village became concerned at the smell of rotting flesh that pervaded their homes one summer. Eventually members of the local police force trawled the woods above the village in search of a body. What they did find were hundreds of stinkhorns.

Flies removing the last of the gleba from a stinkhorn

A Word in your Ear

If ever a mushroom had problems because of its name, this is it. From medieval times both its scientific and common names have linked it to the belief that Judas Iscariot was so ashamed at his betrayal of Jesus that he hanged himself from an elder tree. One early account of this story was:

Judas he japed
With jewen silver
And sithen on an eller
Hanged hymselve.
(*Piers Plowman*)

Jew's ear is one of the largest and most distinctive members of a group of fungi known as the jelly fungi. Its fruitbody, initially smooth and cup-shaped, soon elongates and takes on a size and shape comparable to that of a human ear. Under damp conditions it has a gelatinous, soft, rubbery texture. The outer/upper surface is date brown in colour and slightly velvety; the inner/lower surface is more glossy, reddish purple and convoluted into vein-like wrinkles. When dry the fruitbody shrinks, darkens to a grey–black colour, and becomes tough and horny. It is attached by a small stalk-like region to living or dead wood. In over 90% of records elder is the tree on which the fungus is observed. The ears are all that is left to remind us of Judas's supposed fate.

'*Auricula*' is the Latin word for an ear, while '*Judae*' meant of Judas, from which we get the specific name *auricula-judae*. The fungus is currently placed in the genus *Auricularia* so its full scientific name is *Auricularia auricula-judae* which, like the fungus, is a bit of a mouthful. Since the development by Linnaeus of the binomial system for the scientific names of plants (and fungi), the names have consisted of no more (or less) than two words. The taxonomists who christened this fungus used three words, but managed to bend the rules by hyphenating the last two and thus kept within the letter of the law.

FACING PAGE: Cluster of jew's ear fungus growing on elder

It was previously known as *Hirneola auricula-judae*. In the 18th century it was placed in the genus *Tremella*, but this is now reserved for fungi that parasitise other fungi, as is

the case with the yellow brain fungus (*Tremella mesenterica*), commonly found on burnt gorse. By contrast, *Auricularia* is a saprophyte (on dead wood) or weak parasite (on living wood). It normally grows on the older parts of elder trees, otherwise known as elder elder! Shakespeare was aware of the link between Judas and elder, if not of the fungus, as is evident in *Love's Labour's Lost*, Act V, Scene II:

HOLOFERNES: *(As Judas) Judas I am-*
DUMAINE: *A Judas?*
HOLOFERNES: *Not of scariot, sir.*
(As Judas) Judas I am, yclept Maccabeus.
DUMAINE: *Judas Maccabaeus clipt, is plain Judas.*
BIRON: *A kissing traitor. How art thou prov'd Judas?*
HOLOFERNES: *'Judas I am'*
DUMAINE: *The more shame for you, Judas*
HOLOFERNES: *What mean you, sir?*
BOYET: *To make Judas hang himself.*
HOLOFERNES: *Begin, sir; you are my elder.*
BIRON: *Well followed: Judas was hanged on an elder.*

The name Judas's ear was later shortened to Judas ear, in a manner similar to the change of orchis to orchid; orchids is a much tidier word than orchises. Judas ear was, by late Victorian times, corrupted still further to Jew's ear and this was the name by which the fungus was known throughout the 20th century. The *List of Recommended English Names for Fungi*, published in 2003, suggests yet another change of name, this time to jelly ear. I consider this to be the result of political correctness where it is not necessary. Anti-Semitism was rife in Britain for many centuries, as is evident in the antics of Shylock in another of Shakespeare's plays, but the derogatory term 'Jew's meat', used to describe edible fungi, had nothing to do with Judas's ear. One Victorian writer recorded, 'It has never been regarded here as an edible fungus ...'. The name Jew's ear is a reminder of the folklore surrounding Judas (himself a Jew) and his supposed demise on an elder tree. I for one will continue to call it Jew's ear.

The old herbalists listed the mushroom under yet another term, 'fungus sambuci'; *Sambucus nigra* is the scientific name of elder. Jew's ear was used both as a palliative for sore throats and for its astringent properties (see page 170). Pechey, writing in 1694, says:

> *It grows to the Trunk of the Elder-Tree. Being dried it will keep a good year. Boyl'd in Milk, or infus'd in Vinegar, 'tis good to gargle the Mouth or Throat in Quinsies, and other Inflammations of the Mouth and Throat. And being infus'd in some proper Water, it is good in Diseases of the Eyes.*

Its reputation as an edible fungus has not been held in high esteem in Britain; it was once likened to eating an India rubber with bones in it. It also has a habit of jumping out of a hot pan in a manner akin to popcorn; being hit in the eye by a fungus covered in boiling butter is no fun. In contrast, a very close relative known as wood ear, *Auricularia cornea*, has been cultivated in China for over 1,300 years and is used extensively in Chinese, Japanese and Taiwanese cuisine, especially in soups and stirfries.

Although some books state that Jew's ear is restricted to growing on elder, this is not true. In recent years I have recorded it on sycamore, beech, ash and spindle. I was also once sent a very clear photograph showing it fruiting on the draining board of an old office sink in Hatton Garden. The board, made of sycamore, produced a fine crop. To my knowledge it was not made into a stirfry.

Tippler's Bane

Here is another fungus that, like Jew's ear, has problems with its nomenclature. Older mycologists will know it as common ink cap, but in an attempt to create standardised English names there has been a rejection of most names of more than two words. The result is common inkcap (*Coprinus atramentarius*). The second problem is that although it is common, there is a closely related species which is larger, more conspicuous and more common. This is shaggy inkcap (*Coprinus comatus*), also known as shaggy mane or lawyer's wig. Common inkcap was formerly known as the inky mushroom or inky cap. In North America it goes under the intriguing names of tippler's bane and alcohol inky cap.

Common inkcap is a woodland and garden species with fruitbodies that grow in tufts on the decayed wood of broadleaved tree stumps. It also feeds on buried wood, so the fruitbodies may occur on lawns or near the edge of playing fields. Its broadly bell-shaped, pale grey–brown caps are up to 7 cm high and 5–6 cm across. The faintly striated cap is widest at its base, where its scalloped margin splits at maturity. The crowded white gills age to black before liquefying to ink-like drops at the cap margin. Inkcaps, both common and shaggy, live up to their name as they were formerly used to make an ink substitute (see page 159). Unusually, fruitbodies of common inkcap can be found throughout the year.

Shaggy inkcap prefers disturbed ground or soil containing woody debris. It frequents roadside verges, lawns (especially in new developments where builders have disposed of wood offcuts), playing fields and rubbish tips. It is common in urban situations, where it may occur in large numbers, usually from April to November. When immature, the torpedo-shaped cap conceals its slender stem. The cap is narrowest at the base and covered with tiers of shaggy white scales, akin to a lawyer's wig. Its white gills change to rosy pink before blackening. On maturity the stem may reach up to 30 cm, but by this time much of the cap will have liquefied into a black inky mass.

Chapter 6 of Cooke's *British Edible Fungi – How to Distinguish and how to Cook Them* (1891) was dedicated to inkcaps. Cooke extolled the virtues of shaggy inkcap, despite being cautioned by 'the natives' (the rural population) that they were 'nasty toadstools'.

FACING PAGE: Common inkcap living up to its name

He compares the flavour with that of field mushroom and declares it to be quite equal, if not superior. Shaggy inkcap is still considered by many to be a good edible species with a fine salty flavour. Young specimens need to be fried, baked or grilled on a high heat for a short time only, preferably with a minimum of oil to ensure a crisp texture. Shaggy inkcap is especially good on ciabatta or as a pizza topping. Slow-cooked older specimens have the consistency of hot slugs, but can be gently simmered and then liquidised, making an excellent, if rather grey-coloured soup. They can also be made into 'catsup', a mushroom ketchup.

The edible qualities of common inkcap or inky mushroom were compared by Cooke with those of their shaggy neighbour:

> *There is another fungus, closely related to the above (shaggy caps), and resembling it in many particulars, which is equally edible, and nearly equal to it in flavour.*
>
> *Perhaps more than any other this is the victim of spiteful molestation by small boys and uneducated peasantry, for every exposed cluster is sure to be kicked about and destroyed almost as soon as it appears above ground. The reason for this may be found in the popular belief that it is a poisonous toadstool.*

So Cooke declared common inkcap to be edible, despite the popular belief that it was poisonous. Twenty years later the Ministry of Agriculture and Fisheries' Bulletin No. 23 – *Edible and Poisonous Fungi* – commended the eating of 'shaggy caps' and mentioned common ink cap, but made no comment on its edibility. Edward Step included it as an edible species. By the 1950s, when John Ramsbottom wrote the New Naturalist *Mushrooms and Toadstools*, it was evident that common inkcap was not such a safe edible species as its shaggy relative. Writing of *Coprinus atramentarius* he says that it:

> *shows selection in its manifestations, for some people there is a strange effect if wine or other alcoholic drink is taken at a meal which includes it.*

It is interesting that Cooke did not discover this effect, for although he was an ardent teetotaller in his youth he was fond of a drink in later life. There is some anecdotal evidence that not everyone is affected. Oddly, Jane Grigson's *The Mushroom Feast* (1975) advises 'Do not drink alcohol before, with or after eating shaggy caps', but makes no mention of common inkcap.

The interaction between alcohol (itself a fungal product) and the common inkcap (there is no problem with the shaggy inkcap) was not fully realised until the 1930s. Symptoms include nausea, flushing of the face, headache, a metallic taste in the mouth and, most alarmingly, palpitations and a rapid heart rate. Typically the effects are unpleasant rather than life threatening. Depending on the amount of alcohol drunk, symptoms can last for up to 8 hours and will recur if more alcohol is consumed. These symptoms develop within 5–10 minutes of alcohol intake by a person who has consumed common inkcaps up to 3 days previously. This last point undermines those accounts that only warn about not consuming alcohol *with* the mushrooms: it is definitely a species that should be consumed only by teetotallers.

The toxic compound in common inkcap is known as coprine and despite many assertions to the contrary it is not the same chemical as disulfiram (trade name Antabuse) used in the treatment of alcoholics. It does, however, work in the same way as Antabuse by preventing the breakdown of acetaldehyde (a product of alcohol metabolism) to acetate. The resulting accumulation of acetaldehyde in the blood upsets the autonomic nervous system, producing the symptoms outlined above.

In summary:

Common inkcaps do not choose
If you like a glass of booze.
Try the shaggy ones instead
This will keep you clear of head.

A final word of warning to mushroom hunters: two other common species that can easily be confused with good edible fungi by the novice mycophile have also been implicated as ones to avoid mixing with alcohol. One is lurid bolete (*Boletus luridus*) which, unlike its close relative, the cep, has orange red pores and tubes that turn blue when damaged. The other is club foot (*Ampulloclitocybe clavipes*), a funnel-shaped toadstool of heaths and woodlands occasionally confused with the edible miller (*Clitopilus prunulus*); the latter lacks the swollen stem base of club foot and has a distinctive smell of flour. In North America the club foot goes under the more salutary name of alcohol funnel cap. American reports indicate that it reacts more strongly with whiskey than with other spirits; volunteers are required to test this theory!

Crockery on the Beach

On my bookshelves is a slim volume entitled *Edible Fungi* by W. H. Cobb. The book first appeared in the same year that I did: 1946. Included among the 17 edible species is what Cobb called beech tuft, a fungus that has had more than its fair share of common names, including poached egg fungus, slimy beech cap and porcelain agaric. The current suggested English name is porcelain fungus. Its old names provide useful information. It grows in clusters, typically on older or dead branches of beech trees, and its creamy white cap does look remarkably like a poached egg. The cap surface is slimy and sticky and, unusually for a fungus that grows on trees, it is a gill-bearing agaric (mushroom-shaped). When the sun shines through the cap it looks as if it is made of porcelain.

The scientific name has also changed over the years. It was originally known as *Agaricus mucidus*, Cobb has it as *Armillaria mucida* and it is currently called *Oudemansiella mucida*, in honour of a Dutch botanist named Oudemans. It is frequent in Britain wherever beech is present and as a result is more common in southern England, especially in places such as the New Forest. As an edible species it is coming back into fashion, but it requires slow cooking and the removal of its slimy cap-covering. Artists, potters and photographers have found it a great source of inspiration.

I first found the porcelain fungus in the late 1970s when visiting a friend whose family lived on a large farm near Armagh. After a late night quaffing copious quantities of Guinness and Bushmills, I awoke the following morning to a glorious sunny day and a severe hangover. As a much needed tonic I went for a walk with my camera. Later, as I was admiring an old beech tree, I observed the rays of sun filtering through a tuft of toadstools growing on a branch above my head. When my film was developed I confirmed that I had found porcelain fungus. In my hung over state I had pressed the shutter 36 times, I had a whole film of porcelain.

Ten years later I was asked to lead a fungal foray as part of a residential conference that was being held in the Peak District. The conference delegates worked for AstraZeneca (previously part of ICI) and were in the final stages of testing a novel group of fungicides based on chemicals known as oudemansins and strobilurins. These had

FACING PAGE: Porcelain fungus – *Oudemansiella mucida*, seen from below

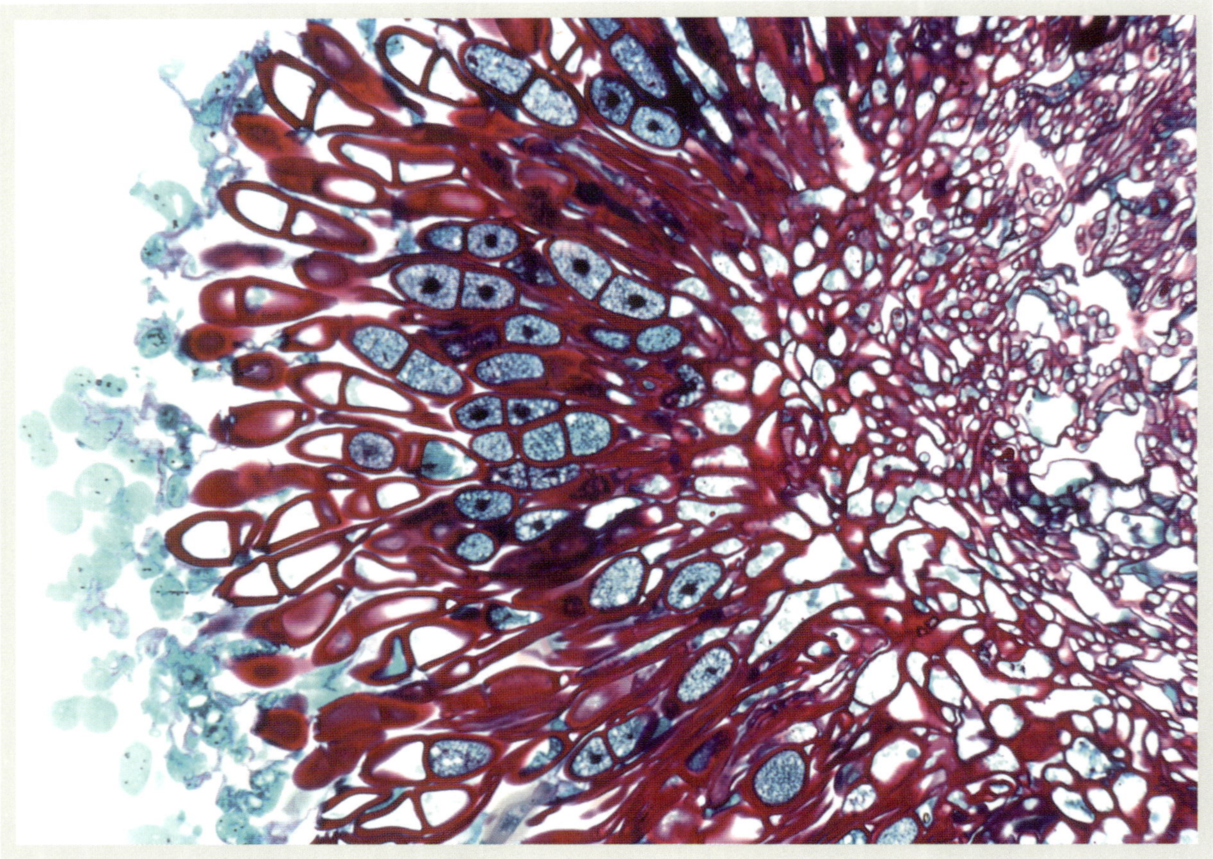

Hollyhock rust

been discovered in the 1960s as products secreted by a number of wood-rotting fungi including porcelain fungus and *Strobilurus tenacellus*, commonly known as pinecone cap (it grows on rotting pine cones). Research had shown that oudemansins and stobilurins restricted the growth of other fungi, presumably giving a competitive advantage to the producing species.

The chemists at the conference had succeeded in making a synthetic strobilurin which is more stable than the natural compounds and has a chemical formula of $C_{22}H_{17}N_3O_5$. In my illustrated lecture to the delegates I showed a slide of porcelain fungus from my Armagh adventure and joked that it might make a good image for their marketing department. Three weeks later I sold the picture and it was widely used in the initial publicity for Amistar, one of several brand names of the new product Azoxystrobin, which was launched in 1988. Hangovers are not usually so profitable.

Azoxystrobin acts by inhibiting the growth of both fungal spores and mycelia by restricting the fungus's energy supply. Unusually, it works on a wide range of different fungal groups including powdery mildews, downy mildews, blasts and rusts: the last group results in significant loss of yields in cereal crops. As I write a new cereal rust has just spread from Africa to Aisa. Worldwide crop yields are reduced by about 20% because of fungal diseases. The product is systemic (it is transported within plants to which it has been applied) and, unlike many previous fungicides, it has relatively low levels of toxicity to other organisms.

Within 12 years of its launch Azoxystrobin had become the leading broad-spectrum fungicide in the world, with sales grossing more than $400 million per annum. The fungicide is extensively used to protect cereals, especially wheat and rice, as well as potatoes, tomatoes, cucumbers, broccoli, grapes and strawberries. Sadly, by 1998 the first signs of resistance to the chemical (by rust fungi on cereals) were reported. In Japan by 2000 there was widespread resistance among fungi attacking cucumber plants.

The evolution of resistance to the new chemical developed by a number of fungal pathogens has necessitated the use of a mixture of different fungicides to maintain crop yields. In the vast and complex world of the fungal kingdom it is probable that other chemicals produced by fungi will form the basis for fungicides of the future.

Foresters have made use of inhibiting chemicals produced by some fungi in attempts to reduce losses from other fungi that parasitise trees. The highly destructive root fomes (*Heterobasidion annosum*) is a fungus that infects the stumps of felled conifers, from where it spreads to attack and kill nearby living conifers. A harmless wood-rotting fungus, *Phlebiopsis gigantea*, which only grows on the dead wood of conifers (where it forms layers looking like sheets of melted candle wax), has been found to inhibit the growth of root fomes. *Phlebiopsis* acts as a biocontrol agent when it is inoculated onto freshly cut conifer stumps and subsequently prevents colonisation of the stumps by the virulently pathogenic root fomes.

All in the Name

Death cap (*Amanita phalloides*) is the most infamous poisonous fungus in Europe, where it is reputed to be responsible for about 90% of all deaths due to toadstool poisoning. Advances in the medical treatment of patients who have ingested the fungus have reduced the death rate from over 60% to between 5 and 20%, but those who do recover are frequently left with severe liver damage along with kidney malfunction. There are three main reasons as to why death cap is implicated in so many deaths. First, it can be confused with a number of edible species; secondly, it is very variable in its cap colour; and finally, a single cap contains enough poison to kill up to eight people.

Death cap, like its other *Amanita* relatives, is a fungus that is mycorrhizal (see page 53) with trees. In Britain it is more frequent in the south, especially with beech or oak on calcareous loam soils. Other well-known amanitas include the hallucinogenic fly agaric (*Amanita muscaria*) (see page 147). Panther cap (*Amanita pantherina*) and destroying angel (*Amanita virosa*) are as poisonous as death cap, but the former is unlike any edible species and the latter is rarely encountered in Britain by the casual mushroom hunter.

One amanita, common in southern Europe, has not yet been recorded in Britain. It is prized as an edible species and was highly sought after in classical Roman times, hence its name: Caesar's mushroom (*Amanita caesarea*). It has a scarlet, unspotted cap and pale yellow gills and was implicated in one of the most famous poisonings attributed to death cap: the death of the Emperor Claudius Caesar. When Claudius married his fourth wife, Agrippina, she already had a son, Nero, and the two of them plotted to ensure that Nero, not Claudius's son Britannicus, would succeed as Emperor. At a banquet at which a dish of Caesar's mushroom was served it is believed that Claudius's portion was laced with juice extracted from death cap. Claudius died and Nero became Emperor thanks to a plot that was rather more subtle than a knife in the back.

Two other deaths of famous people have been blamed on death cap: Pope Clement VII and the Austrian King Charles VI. As the former died from an illness lasting for 5 months this does not indicate poisoning by death cap, but the latter is said to have suffered indigestion after eating sautéed mushrooms and to have died 10 days later.

FACING PAGE:
Death cap – *Amanita phalloides*

This is very much the time-scale for death by *Amanita phalloides*. As head of the Austrian branch of the house of Habsburg, his death in October 1740 led to the War of Austrian Succession and prompted the comment by Voltaire that:

> *this dish of mushrooms changed the destiny of Europe.*

The amanitas are woodland fungi and have several features in common. They fruit from mid-summer onwards and have gills (usually white like the spore colour) that are not attached to the top of the stem. The young fruitbody bursts from a veil like a bird hatching from an egg. Very young *Amanita* fruitbodies resemble puffballs from the outside, but cutting in half will reveal the enclosed cap and stem hidden within. The bottom of the veil, known as a volva, remains as a sac or 'egg-cup' surrounding the stem base. Death cap is distinguished by its slightly shiny, olive–green cap, streaked with darker radiating fibres, and a white ring on a white stem, the base of which is enclosed in a sac-like volva. The convex young cap later flattens and expands to 10–12 cm across; it may be more yellow–brown or even off-white and is only rarely topped by remnants of the white veil. It has a faint, sweet odour, akin to rose petals.

Apart from the amanitas very few other fungi have a basal volva. This is why my advice to anyone who collects wild fungi for gastronomic reasons is *not* to cut through the stem base as a means of gathering specimens; a method recommended by some authors. Anyone gathering 'mushrooms' in this way runs the risk of leaving the highly diagnostic volva in the ground. Sadly, for one American family of Korean immigrants, on a chestnut picking excursion, the presence of the death cap's volva reminded them of their own culture's edible paddy straw mushroom (*Volvariella volvacea*) which although not an amanita, also has a distinctive volva. The family of five ate large quantities of the death caps they collected and all became seriously ill; four of them required liver transplants.

A slightly smaller amanita, the false death cap (*Amanita citrina*), is much more common in Britain and is frequently mistaken for the true death cap. As the Latin name implies, the cap is typically citrus lemon-yellow (but can be white) and is often covered with patches of the veil. The volva is more like an egg-cup than a bag and the fungus has a very strong smell of raw potatoes or radish. False death cap is not poisonous.

The similarity of the two species almost derailed the murderous intentions of a French serial killer, a certain Monsieur Girard, in the early part of the 20th century.

Along with his wife and mistress, Girard impersonated wealthy acquaintances at medical examinations required for the instigation of their life insurance policies, paid for by Girard, in which he was the sole beneficiary. He hired a man to collect fungi with white gills, a ring on the stem and a volva, and these were served to the insured guests at lavish dinner parties. Some of the intended victims survived, because Girard did not recognise the false death caps that his unwitting accomplice occasionally collected. Following the death of one woman on whose life Girard had taken out policies with four different companies only 3 weeks earlier, one doctor became suspicious and on inspecting the corpse found that it was not the same person that he had examined some weeks before. Girard was executed for murder in 1918. His wife and mistress served life sentences.

Destroying angel
Amanita virosa

The initial symptom associated with most mushroom poisoning consists of gastrointestinal pain within 6 hours of ingestion. The first symptoms of poisoning by death cap do not manifest themselves until between 8 and 12 hours after ingestion, and for low doses the delay may be as much as 36 hours. This long delay makes use of a stomach pump futile, as the mushroom has already been digested. Intense abdominal pain, coupled with vomiting and severe diarrhoea, can lead to dehydration and require hospital treatment, but the symptoms usually subside after about 24 hours. This 'honeymoon' period may even result in the patient being discharged, but about 48 hours later the pain returns and with it signs of jaundice, blood in the stools, delirium and coma due to low blood sugar levels. Along with liver failure there is also evidence of kidney malfunction. This can result in death 7 to 10 days after the first symptoms.

Survival is enhanced by fluid replacement, activated charcoal (to absorb the poison), intravenous glucose and attempts to limit liver damage with intravenous penicillin G and extracts of milk thistle (*Silybum marianum*). The toxin responsible for most of the symptoms is alpha-amanitin. This inhibits protein synthesis and results in the death of liver cells, initiating liver and renal failure. A dose as little as 5 mg is sufficient to kill an adult. Toxicity is not reduced by freezing or cooking.

Fatalities from death cap are not uncommon in parts of central and northern Europe, but figures for England and Wales indicate that there were just 39 deaths between 1920 and 1950. Since then the annual number of fatalities in Britain has declined, with just 11 poisonings by death cap between 1973 and 1981, only one of which was fatal. Both here and in North America the frequency and severity of mushroom poisoning are often exaggerated by the media.

Many of the earlier victims were misled by the ease with which the skin of the death cap can be peeled off. The old wives' tale that only the skin of edible mushrooms could be peeled was widely believed. The late Lord Deedes reiterated this in his *Daily Telegraph* column in 2006, but his error was quickly rebuked by a worried correspondent. Ironically, poisonings from death cap in North America are on the increase. While many of the victims, like the Koreans mentioned above, have been immigrants, it also appears that death cap may have been introduced to the United States between the two World Wars and is still spreading.

St Anthony's Fire

It is a widely held tenet among historians that the world's great civilisations all relied on cereal crops as a principal source of food. These included wheat, barley, oats, rye, maize and rice; all members of the grass family. Given that supplies of meat and milk from grazing domesticated animals are also dependent on grasses from pasture, hay or silage, it is difficult to overestimate humankind's debt to the grass family. Many species of mushroom and toadstool, including the field mushroom (*Agaricus campestris*), make their home in grassland habitats, but grasses and cereals also play host to a number of parasitic microfungi. Foremost among these are the rust fungi (so called because they often produce rust-coloured patches on the leaves of their host plants), of which over 7,000 species are known, growing on a wide range of different plant species.

That people have had to put up with cereal fungal pests for thousands of years is hinted at in Genesis 41: 25–27:

> *Then Joseph said to Pharaoh, 'The dream of Pharaoh is one; God has revealed to Pharaoh what he is about to do'. The seven good cows are seven years, and the seven good ears are seven years; the dream is one. The seven lean and gaunt cows that come up after them are seven years, and the seven empty ears blighted by the east wind are also seven years of famine.*

In Britain westerly winds are the chief rain-bringers, but in the Middle East (particularly during the cooler, wetter conditions of 4,000 years ago), easterly winds bring rain. Like other fungi, rusts prefer damp conditions. Winds may also introduce initial infection as rust spores can travel for thousands of miles, on the wind. The cultivation of wheat, barley, oats and rye appears to have started in the Middle East and it is very likely that the blighted ears of grain mentioned in Genesis were caused by a fungal rust disease in the genus *Puccinia*.

Pliny attributed frost damage to 'the greatest pest of the crops' when writing about a disease of wheat, but its fungal origin is strongly hinted at by the action of placing laurel leaves in the fields, 'for then the rust passed from the wheat onto the laurel leaves'. Many

QVELE POL
ASTRE SONO
DI S. ANTONIO
MIRACOLO DI S. ANTONIO FVORA DI BRESIA

St Anthony

rust diseases infect different plant species at different stages of their life cycle. The Romans, finding this treatment ineffective, resorted to calling for help from the god Robigus (from the Latin word *robigo*, meaning blight). The resulting ceremony included the sacrifice of a rusty-coloured dog; sadly to no avail.

Rusts are classified in the Basidiomycete group of fungi, along with mushrooms and toadstools. Another scourge of cereal crops belongs in the Ascomycete group, alongside fungi such as morels and dead man's fingers (*Xylaria polymorpha*). The fungus concerned is *Claviceps purpurea*, commonly known (as is the plant disease it causes) as ergot. It parasitises the flowers of members of the grass family, including many cereal crops. The word ergot comes from the old French *argot*, meaning a cockerel's spur which, like the fungus, is slightly curved. Ergot resembles a tiny, hard, purple–black banana that is typically no more than 2 cm long and just 2 mm in diameter.

Unlike species of mushroom and toadstool which are identified by their fruitbodies, ergot is recognised by the curving black structure. This is a resting organ known as a sclerotium. It is produced in the flower head, from the ovary of an infected plant at the same time as uninfected ovaries are producing the grain-like seeds typical of the grass family. An Assyrian tablet from the 6th century BC describes a 'noxious pustule in the ear of grain', while a European account written in 1582 describes the long, black, hard, narrow 'corn pegs' protruding like long nails between the grains. At the time neither the pustules nor pegs were thought to be of fungal origin. 'Corn' in this context refers to rye; the American corn or maize had not yet been introduced to Europe.

A fungal link was mooted during the 1700s, but not firmly established until the 1800s. Even so, the pegs were initially looked on merely as a symptom of the problem. It was not until Berkeley's investigation in 1846 of what we now call potato blight, that it was realised that fungi could be the cause and not just one result of a plant disease.

In a manner similar to plant seeds, the sclerotia (pegs) fall to the ground in the late summer and remain dormant over the winter. In late spring they produce up to a dozen tiny, spore-bearing fruitbodies, resembling minute, pink-headed drumsticks. These release thread-like, wind-borne sexual spores. Any that land on the stigmas of cereal flowers germinate to produce a hyphal tube that invades the ovary. Here, food produced by the plant to swell its seeds (grain) is used instead to produce fungal tissue. The fungus produces masses of asexual spores along with a sweet 'honeydew'. The spores are carried to surrounding plants both by rain splash and by flies and other insects, attracted to the nectar-like honeydew. Later in the summer new sclerotia are produced and the fungal life cycle is complete.

Cereal crops infected with ergot suffer a loss in grain yield as ovaries producing ergots do not produce seeds. In addition, the fungus can cause sterility in the surrounding flowers of the cereal 'ear'. Sadly, this yield loss is nothing compared to the problems resulting from the ingestion of ergot-contaminated grain. When cereals are harvested the grain, along with any ergot, is thrashed from the plants. Most of the grain earmarked for human food (as opposed to animal food or alcohol production) is milled to make flour. Archaeological finds have indicated that some European grain samples of the medieval period contained as much as a third, by volume, of ergot.

The resultant grey flour was largely scorned by the well-off who could afford better quality (white) flour, sourced from uninfected crops. It was mostly the poor who suffered what we now call ergotism, as a result of eating ergot-contaminated flour. One of the earliest documented accounts of what is assumed to be ergotism comes from Germany in AD 857:

> *A great plague of swollen blisters consumed the people by a loathsome rot, so that their limbs were loosened and fell off before death.*

Later records indicated that the disease manifested itself in two different ways: gangrenous ergotism, as exemplified above, and convulsive ergotism. Oddly, episodes of the former were mostly found in France and areas to the west of the Rhine, with convulsive ergotism occurring in the rest of Europe (including Britain) and also in North America. Initial symptoms of gangrenous ergotism include the feeling of intense heat, especially at or near limb extremities.

In the 10th century victims of a 'plague of fire' near Paris were cared for at a local church. The bread they were given came from uncontaminated flour and many recovered, giving rise to the belief that *ignis sacer* (holy fire) was the result of divine retribution. A hospital dedicated to St Anthony also successfully treated many sufferers and in 1093 the Order of St Anthony was established. This initiated the building of churches dedicated to the saint, to whom sufferers prayed for redemption from what became known as St Anthony's fire. St Anthony was a 4th century Christian hermit who lived in Egypt and became a role model for pious Catholics throughout Europe. He was believed to have power over fire and flame.

The symptoms of convulsive ergotism include muscular twitching and seizures resembling those of epileptics, so much so that it may lie behind medieval dancing manias. Later, patients were diagnosed as being afflicted with St Vitus's dance. Many sufferers experience hallucinations and formication, the sensation that ants are running about under the skin. Climate, soil type and different cereal strains have all been cited as reasons for the two types of ergotism. Both forms frequently result in death, especially among children who, largely as a result of lower body mass, are more sensitive to the poisons found in ergot.

These poisons include a number of alkaloids (a group of chemicals also found in plants such as deadly nightshade and hemlock) including ergotamine which restrict blood flow to certain parts of the body. Those parts that are starved of blood, typically extremities including hands and feet, dry up and turn black before falling off, often in the absence of pain and bleeding. Other ergot alkaloids, including a derivative of lysergic acid, cause symptoms associated with convulsive ergotism. The alkaloid ergometrine causes spontaneous abortions, but has also been used to help with childbirth (see page 176). As ergot is also found on grasses, ergometrine has probably had an important effect on the availability of both milk and meat by reducing the reproductive activity of livestock.

Ergot on rye

Of all cereals, rye is the one most prone to infection by ergot. In 1989 Mary Matossian published the results of her historical research linking the prevalence of witchcraft trials to rye-growing areas of Europe. The Irish, who relied on potatoes rather than cereals, have only one recorded witchcraft trial, but East Anglia, which grew considerable amounts of rye, was the setting for some serious witch hunting, especially in the 16th century. In her book *Poisons of the Past*, Matossian shows that the number of witchcraft trials rose following cool, wet springs; conditions that favour the spread of ergot.

The most famous witch trial, immortalised in Arthur Miller's play *The Crucible*, was not in Europe but in Salem, New England, in 1692. The founding fathers in this region had bought seeds of rye from England to grow as a crop to provide them with their daily bread. Diary records indicate that the community suffered from unusually cold spring weather in the early 1690s, which would have favoured the spread of ergot. Symptoms of the 'bewitched', mostly women and children, included pricking sensations, hallucinations and convulsive seizures; all features of ergotism. Ironically, had the New Englanders grown maize, the staple cereal of Central and North America, there would have been no problem as ergot does not infect maize.

Since the link was made between the symptoms described above and the ergot fungus in the 18th century the incidence of ergotism has been largely eradicated in the Western world. Plant breeding for increased resistance, backed by chemical sprays and, most importantly, the separation of grain and fungus by flotation, has been aided by deep ploughing which buries the over-wintering sclerotia. Despite these precautions there was a severe outbreak of ergotism during the 1950s in France.

Given the symptoms of ergotism one would not expect to find evidence of the deliberate ingestion of the fungus, other than in carefully controlled medical preparations (see page 176). History suggests, however, that this may have been the case thousands of years ago among the Ancient Greeks. According to Greek mythology, Persephone, the daughter of Demeter (the goddess of agriculture), was kidnapped and taken to the Underworld to be the wife of Hades. In her grief Demeter sent a famine which was broken by Zeus's arrangement that Persephone only spend a third of the year in the Underworld. During the 8 months shared with her daughter, Demeter provided suitable growing conditions and for many years in October the Greeks performed a form of harvest festival by re-enacting the story of the reunification between Demeter and her daughter.

The celebrations known as the Lesser Mysteries started in Athens, but later decamped to the small town of Eleusis, about 10 miles away. Here only a select few were allowed to cross the River Kephisos and enter the temple of Demeter to partake of the Greater Mysteries. Participants, including Homer, Plato and Socrates, were sworn to secrecy not to reveal their experiences, but some information leaked out. The ritual revolved around the drinking of *kykeon*, a purple potion made from meal which resulted in tremors, hallucinations, profuse sweating and feelings of fear. If *kykeon* was a form of beer it seems unlikely that a low-grade alcohol alone would produce such symptoms. There is no evidence that the ancient Greeks had learnt the art of distilling, which results in a much higher alcohol content.

Perhaps the clue lies in the colour: ground ergot sclerotia turn water purple. If the grain used to make *kykeon* was deliberately chosen because it contained ergot then the resulting alkaloids in the potion would have readily accounted for the experiences recounted by those who partook of the Mysteries. Perhaps the fungus-induced visions experienced by men such as Plato and Socrates even had a bearing on the history of philosophy.

Many years later, in the 1940s, the Swiss pharmaceutical firm Sandoz investigated a range of chemicals found in ergot during a search for potential medicinal drugs. One of the drugs, lysergic acid, is the basis for a range of lysergic acid derivatives and in 1943 one of the firm's chemists was re-examining the properties of D-lysergic diethylamide, or LSD for short. Albert Hofmann later described his experiences when he accidentally ingested a tiny amount of what we now know is a very powerful psychoactive drug. He was cycling home when he began seeing colours and had a wonderful feeling:

> *It gave me inner joy and peace. It opened my eyes to the miracle of creation.*

The rest, as they say, is history. The influence of LSD on literature is outlined on page 198, but it was also widely used during the 1950s in psychiatry and has been a major component of the drug culture since the 1960s. In January 2006 Albert Hofmann celebrated his 100th birthday, calling LSD 'my wonderful child and my problem child'. Without it Lucy would never have ventured into the Sky with Diamonds.

petroleū

Mushroom Magic

In certain parts of the world there is a wealth of historical evidence showing the importance of certain psychotropic (mind-altering) fungi used in ritual, magical and religious ceremonies, as well as for pleasure. The species involved are now usually referred to as hallucinogenic or magic mushrooms. The most famous of these include fly agaric (*Amanita muscaria*) and a range of small toadstools, mostly in the genus *Psilocybe*, that contain the active compound psilocybin. Note that the *P* is silent, like the ones in swimming pools! Prior to the 1970s mycophobic Britain, unlike Asia, North and Central America and other parts of Europe, had little or no folklore surrounding the deliberate ingestion of hallucinogenic mushrooms.

By the 16th century Europeans used alcohol (in many different forms) as a source of social inebriation but, with the notable exception of the Christian Church's sacramental wine, alcohol played no significant part in religious ceremonies. The army of the Spanish Conquistadors that overran the countries of Central America in the latter half of the 16th century were accompanied by Catholic priests. Their presence was ostensibly to spread the faith and chronicle events in the new colony, but also to ensure that the Church shared in the booty.

Numerous descriptions, including those by Spanish Dominican and Franciscan priests, detail aspects of the Aztec civilisation that was so brutally suppressed by the invaders from the Old World. Their reports include examples of cannibalism, human sacrifices, and the ritual and religious use of various non-alcoholic inebriants. These included preparations made from the seeds of morning glory, the peyote cactus and, most importantly, hallucinogenic mushrooms known as *teonanácatl*, meaning flesh of the gods.

> *At a banquet the first thing the Indians ate, was a black mushroom. These mushrooms caused them to become intoxicated, to see visions and also to be provoked to lust. They ate the mushrooms with honey and when they began to feel excited due to the effect of the mushrooms, the Indians started dancing, while some were singing and others weeping.*
>
> (*Florentine Codex*)

FACING PAGE: *Simple Medicines* by Mattheaus Platearius *c.* 1470

The Spanish were determined to eliminate all vestiges of Aztec religious culture. They looked on the Aztec gods and the sacred mushrooms as creators of the Devil. At first all that happened was a strange fusion, as described in a 17th century account of a service to honour a Catholic saint. The saint's image was present on the altar, along with sacred mushrooms and a bowl of fermented agave juice. At the conclusion of the ceremony the participants were offered mushrooms and juice in the manner of the Christian faith's use of bread and wine. Later, however, the use of inebriants in Central America sank out of sight for some 300 years.

In the late 1800s curious stone carvings were discovered in Central America, mostly in Guatemala but also as far north as Mexico. Although some were relatively recent (*c.* 15th century) most came from the Mayan period (AD 317–889) and some dated back to the 1st millennium BC. Originally these carved statuettes were thought to have phallic significance, but 20th century researchers concluded that the figures probably represented mushroom deities and some began to make a link with the 16th century accounts outlined above.

In 1938 an American ethnologist Robert Weitlaner was investigating Amerindian culture in the Oaxaca region of Mexico when he witnessed a curing (healing) ritual. During the course of this, intoxicating mushrooms were consumed by a local Mazatec healer or *curandera*. The practice of using hallucinogenic mushrooms was not dead! The following year some of the mushrooms were collected by an ethnobotanist, Richard Schultes. One was identified as *Stropharia* (*Psilocybe*) *cubensis*, a very potent hallucinogen. It was not until after World War II that more information on the ritual, together with a more accurate determination of the fungal species involved, was obtained.

Enter Gordon Wasson, a retired American banker, along with his Russian-born wife Valentina, who were fascinated with the historical use of hallucinogenic fungi. They had become convinced that hallucinogenic mushrooms had played a crucial role in the evolution of human cultures and religion. In 1953 they accompanied Weitlaner on a trip to southern Mexico. Two years later, Gordon became the first foreigner to consume hallucinogenic mushrooms as part of a Mazatec curing ritual under the guidance of a local *curandera* called Maria Sabina. Soon after this Gordon, together with his wife and daughter, experimented with the mushrooms.

The Wassons collaborated with an eminent French botanist, Roger Heim, who identified the species collected, showing that the most important was *Psilocybe mexicana* (known to the Indians as *Angelito*, little angel). Heim also began to culture the mushrooms in his laboratory, from which Albert Hofmann was able to determine their chemical content. The active compound psilocybin and its associate compound psilocin were first extracted from *Psilocybe mexicana*. Although psilocybin is colourless it turns blue in the presence of oxygen, a feature frequently observed when psilocybin-containing fungi are handled.

Hofmann worked at the Sandoz laboratories in Basle, where, in the course of analysing the chemicals found in the ergot fungus, he had discovered LSD (see page 139), an event that led him to study the chemical nature of other hallucinogens. On 13th January 2006 Hofmann celebrated his centenary before an adoring crowd in Basle. Most of the press reports dwelt on LSD, but Albert was also at the forefront of the mushroom revolution. The CIA was also interested in both LSD and hallucinogenic mushrooms. They provided undercover funding for the Wassons' Mexico visit in 1956, in order that they might obtain mushroom samples.

Structurally, psilocybin and psilocin are very similar (the former is converted to the latter in the human body) and both resemble LSD. All three substances bear structural similarities with the body's neural transmitter chemicals serotonin and dopamine. Much of their action is a result of an effect on the body's autonomic nervous system. Typically, low doses of psilocybin induce relaxation and a sense of detachment, medium doses result in alterations in the dimensions of both time and space, while high doses promote hallucinations that include a distortion in the perception of colour.

In 1957 Gordon Wasson wrote an article about his Mexican research and experiences. This was published in *Life* magazine under the title *Seeking the Magic Mushroom*. The article triggered a veritable avalanche of pilgrims on the unsuspecting Mexican Indians. Among the visitors were serious mycologists and journalists, but also celebrities and later the flower children of the 1960s, many of them seeking an instant way of reaching Nirvana. Wasson, who declared that most of the visitors had been 'riff-raff', was nevertheless a moving force in the rise of what became known as the hippie counterculture.

In 1960 a 40-year-old philosophy professor from Harvard became one more visitor to Mexico to experience magic mushrooms. Timothy Leary later wrote of his experience:

During the next five hours, I was whirled through an experience which could be described in many extravagant metaphors but which was, above all and without question, the deepest religious experience of my life.

Leary's experiments with psilocybin and LSD and his infamous call to fellow Americans to 'tune in, turn on, and drop out' propelled him to the head of the hippie movement, immortalised by the Moody Blues: 'Timothy Leary's dead now ... no, no, he's outside looking in'. One place he was no longer looking in was Harvard, from which he was sacked in 1963.

The Mazatec healer Maria Sabina later wrote of her own consternation: 'Before Wasson nobody took the mushrooms only to find God. They were always taken for the sick to get well'. Despite her misgivings, Maria gave copious information and a supply of mushrooms free of charge to all who called on her. She died in poverty, aged 97, in 1985. Gordon Wasson followed her, aged 88, a year later.

In 1962 Hofmann isolated psilocybin from the small fungus *Psilocybe semilanceata*. Common throughout temperate Europe and North America, it was known as liberty cap on account of the similarity between its cap shape and the symbol of the French revolution. In the mid-1970s a Sheffield mycologist, Rod Cooke, wrote an undergraduate textbook entitled *Fungi, Man and His Environment*. A chapter on hallucinogenic fungi culminated in a final paragraph:

Psilocybe semilanceata, *'liberty caps', is widespread in Europe and other north-temperate zones, and the fruit bodies contain sufficient psilocybin to have a hallucinogenic effect if they are eaten even in small quantities. This fungus is common, occurs in large numbers, is not poisonous, and is distinctive enough not to be confused with other species – yet, apparently, it has never been used even as a casual inebriant.*

By the end of the 1970s liberty caps had become magic mushrooms and the subject of scary headlines in the British media. What may have been a rare example of students reading a textbook was no doubt aided by American exchange students recognising the 'little brown jobs' among the green-field campuses of the new universities of York, Sussex and Lancaster. Aside from university campuses, troops of the mushroom occur from mid-summer to late autumn in unimproved, sheep-grazed pasture land, but also on playing fields and parks. Contrary to popular opinion, *Psilocybe semilanceata* does not grow on animal dung; indeed, I discovered a small colony growing on my own back lawn.

The 1971 Misuse of Drugs act included the chemicals psilocybin and psilocin under class A, but *Psilocybe semilanceata* was not itself outlawed; at the time it was not considered a threat. The legal status of collections and preparations of magic mushrooms remained a grey area until a clarification made by the Home Office in 2002 that it was not an offence to possess, sell or consume freshly picked specimens of *Psilocybe*. The result was an explosion of websites and Amsterdam-style 'shroom' shops all selling 'grow your own' kits, with most offering species originating from Central America.

The result was a 40% increase in the number of people using magic mushrooms. By 2005 the government panicked and the law was changed again. Under the new law 'grow your own' kits and dried mushrooms were made illegal, and there was even a threat to landowners on whose ground the magic mushrooms appeared. It is perhaps ironic that several other previously rare, hallucinogenic species of *Psilocybe*, including the aptly named blueleg brownie *Psilocybe cyanescens*, have started to spread on woodchip mulch (see page 59). Countless gardens, parks, riding stables and children's play areas could yet be in trouble with the law.

Despite Rod Cooke's assertion that liberty caps are too distinctive to be confused with other species this has not proved to be true for some mushroom hunters. They have consumed a range of similar-looking little brown jobs, some of which also contain psilocybin. The main problems associated with the consumption of magic mushrooms seem to be of a psychological nature, and frightened young people frequently turn up at their local accident and emergency unit. Some experience 'flashbacks' in the days following their trip. 'Bad trips' are much more likely when the mushrooms are consumed along with alcohol or other drugs.

To date some 150 species of *Psilocybe* have been identified from every corner of the globe, most of which are associated with agricultural and horticultural habitats. At least 50% of them have been found to be hallucinogenic. A much larger hallucinogenic fungus that is native to Britain and sometimes confused by beginners with honey fungus (see page 108) is the enigmatic spectacular rustgill, *Gymnopilus junonius* (*spectabilis*). Forming clumps of large, bright rusty gold-coloured fruitbodies which release rusty-brown spores, the species is not uncommon on rotting wood. For years authors have argued over whether it is hallucinogenic, but some specimens have been found to contain psilocybin while other samples are free of the drug. In Japan it is known as waraitake or the laughing mushroom on account of its effect. Maybe it will have the last laugh.

A Toadstool is Spotted

With its shiny crimson cap, bearing concentric rings of white, wart-like spots, fly agaric is perhaps the most recognised toadstool in the English-speaking world. It is found in north temperate zones; throughout Britain, across Europe and Eurasia as well as in North America, South Africa and New Zealand. It is frequently depicted in illustrations for fairy stories and on greetings cards as well as in the form of garden ornaments, when it is usually associated with gnomes. I am writing this on St Patrick's Day and the card from my family depicts a shamrock-wearing bear, sitting on a fly agaric. Some people are not even aware that it actually exists, outside an imaginary world, and the majority of the British public are convinced that it is deadly poisonous.

Its scientific name, *Amanita muscaria*, indicates that it is closely related to death cap (*Amanita phalloides*) (see page 129) and destroying angel (*Amanita virosa*), the ingestion of which can indeed prove fatal. Despite assertions by many authors, the consumption of fly agaric has only very rarely resulted in death, the most quoted example dating back to 1893! As we shall see, the toadstool does contain chemicals of a poisonous nature, but these are more likely to produce out-of-body experiences, sickness and diarrhoea, rather than fatalities. As with other amanitas, the young fruitbody is enclosed in a skin-like veil, through which the developing toadstool expands. In fly agaric, the remains of the veil appear as white flecks on the red cap, with a cup-shaped volva at the stem base.

Fly agaric is ectomycorrhizal with trees (see page 53) and in Britain is most commonly associated with birch, whereas in North America, where it also occurs in a form with a white-spotted, yellow–orange cap, it typically grows with pines. The species name *muscaria* comes from the scientific name for the house fly, *Musca domestica*. The common name fly agaric is simply an anglicised version of this, just as with the German *Fliegenpilz* (fly-fungus). The toadstool's link with flies comes from a series of writings dating back to Albertus Magnus in the 13th century. In the 18th century Linnaeus wrote of the pounded fruitbodies being used to kill bedbugs. Many authors have since repeated the premise that the fungi were regularly used as fly-killers, although few have put it to

FACING PAGE:
Frog on a toadstool

the test. It is now known that the fungus contains 1,3-diolein, a compound that flies find irresistible and may cause them to consume extracts of the toxic fungus.

Gordon Wasson who, along with his wife Valentina, had brought the ritual use of Mexican hallucinogenic mushrooms to the attention of the world in 1957, was convinced that hallucinogenic mushrooms had played a crucial role in the evolution of human culture and religion in many parts of the world. Knowing that fly agaric had been consumed for its hallucinogenic effects in parts of Eurasia, they dismissed the fly-killing story as a cover for a toadstool that they suspected was more associated with the fly of madness (as in 'he's got a fly in his ear'), rather than fly killing. For the Wassons (although sadly Valentina died before the conclusion of their studies), *Amanita muscaria* had a much more important role; that of soma, as immortalised in Aldous Huxley's 1932 novel *Brave New World*.

When Gordon Wasson was still working in Wall Street he shared his fungal fascination over lunch with Huxley and proposed that soma might not be a plant, as most scholars believed, but fly agaric. In the 2nd millennium BC a group of Aryans (Indo-Iranians) journeyed south, invading the Indus valley while the rest stayed put in Central Asia. Among the earliest texts of these peoples are the Indian *Rig Veda* (Hindu texts) and the Iranian *Avesta*, both of which feature a 'plant' called soma in the *Rig Veda* and haoma in the *Avesta*, at the centre of an important act of worship. In his classic book *Soma – Divine Mushroom of Immortality*, my copy of which is serendipitously marked 'ex libris Anthony Huxley', Wasson argues that the descriptions and effects of soma and haoma fit those of fly agaric more closely than those of hallucinogenic plants previously put forward as soma/haoma candidates.

Robert Graves was fascinated by the Wassons' work (he partook of the Mexican psilocybe, which he referred to as 'a divine ambrosia') and had second thoughts about Dionysus, and her autumnal feast on Ambrosia, in an updating of his book *The Greek Myths*. He surmised that the antics of Satyrs and Centaurs may in part have been due to consumption of fly agaric. He also mused on the story of Perseus, who named the city of Mycenae after a toadstool that he found growing on the site. The genus *Mycena* includes a large number of our smaller toadstools, one of which, lilac bonnet (*Mycena pura*), is believed to contain muscarine.

While many scholars have refuted Wasson's soma suggestions, his earlier work, co-authored with his wife, on the use of hallucinogenic fly agarics by Eurasian tribes, is still widely regarded. Ironically, Gordon had a typical Anglo-Saxon approach to mushrooms, and when his Russian-born wife Valentina gathered and served wild mushrooms during their first holiday as a married couple, he refused to touch them. She later won him round and together they began to investigate the attitudes to mushrooms shown by, among others, the Slavs, Anglo-Saxons, Lapps and Albanians.

Written reports of inebriation resulting from the ingestion of fly agaric in parts of Siberia and Lapland date back over 300 years. In 1658 a Polish soldier held captive as a prisoner of war in western Siberia noted that the Ostyak peoples did

> *eat certain fungi in the shape of fly agarics, and thus they got drunk worse than on vodka, and for them that's the very best banquet.*

In the following century a colonel in the Swedish army was captured by the Koryak people of eastern Siberia. In 1736 he recorded that fly agarics were items of value, being frequently traded for animal pelts. He also wrote about poorer individuals who were unable to afford the inebriating mushrooms, but waited instead with bowls outside the huts of those who had become intoxicated, and collected their urine. The poor then quaffed the yellow liquor and achieved the same state as those who had eaten the fungi.

A few years later a report of an expedition led by Vitus Bering, to explore the Kamchatka peninsular and Alaska (the Straits between the two now bear his name), included an account of a feast held by the Kamchadales:

> *... sometimes they use a liquor made of a large mushroom, with which the Russians kill flies. This they prepare with the juice of epilobium [willow herb] .... Some jump, some dance, and sing ... A small hole appearing to them a great pit, and a spoonful of water as a lake.*

In the early 19th century Geog Landsdorf also recorded that an inability to judge the size of objects, or people, was a symptom displayed by Kamchadel fly agaric eaters. He noted that vodka had by this time become the more common form of inebriation. One result of this was that they traded most of their fly agarics with the reindeer-herding Koryak tribe. A probable literary result of Mordecai Cooke's attempt to enlighten the British public about the effects of eating fly agaric is recorded on page 201. In addition to reports of fly agaric usage in Siberia and more western parts of Russia there is also historical evidence of similar practices among the reindeer-herding Saami people of Lapland (northern Norway, Finland and Sweden).

The Wassons were less interested in the recreational use of fly agaric and concentrated on its role in shamanistic ritual in both Siberia and Lapland. Use by shamans was said to help them to communicate with spirits, gods and even the dead, in order to explain dreams and heal the sick. One of the Koryak gods was known as Big Raven, the ancestor of men. When Big Raven lacked the strength to return a whale to the sea, he called on the Supreme Being from whose spittle grew fly agarics, the ingestion of which gave Big Raven the strength he needed. A similar story tells of fly agarics sprouting on Christmas night from ground touched by flecks of foam that have fallen from Sleipnir, the horse ridden by the Norse god Wotan.

The Saami people of Lapland have a long tradition of reindeer herding and have made use of fly agarics as an attractant when rounding up the semi-wild, nomadic animals. It appears that reindeer also get high on the toadstool. There are even accounts of reindeer licking the snow made yellow by urinating Saami. While it is tempting to surmise that such animals have learnt that the yellow snow will also make them high, if the donor had eaten fly agarics, it is more likely that urine is providing salt and other useful minerals that will keep the animals firmly on the ground. As for the long-observed habit of humans drinking the urine of 'bemushroomed' individuals, there is a strong argument that this tradition gave rise to the term 'getting pissed', now indicative of an inebriated state caused not by a mushroom, but by alcohol.

Some authors, including me (see *The Christmas Book*, 2007), have argued that the inebriated (ho-ho), red and white suited, gift-bearing Father Christmas, transported by flying reindeer and entering and leaving dwellings by way of the chimney, has as much in common with a Saami shaman as a Catholic saint from Turkey. For Laplanders, late December is a time of permanent darkness, conditions favouring SAD (seasonal affective disorder) resulting in more work for healers.

The shaman, inebriated by the red and white fly agaric, enters the yurt (winter dwelling) with a gift of healing for the sick person within and exits by climbing the pole holding up the roof before departing via the smoke hole. Every child knows that Santa comes from Lapland and like the fly agaric is frequently depicted surrounded by elves. Anyway, whoever saw reindeer in Turkey? The delightful poem, now called *The Night Before Christmas*, written in 1822 by Clement Clarke Moore, introduced the modern

Santa as a mixture of the classical teetotal Saint Nicholas from southern Europe and a more intriguing north European figure pulled by reindeer and taking a mushroom trip.

Fly agarics have featured in other Christian roles aside from Father Christmas. The eve of Christmas, 24th December, is also Adam and Eve's Day. I have long been sceptical about the idea that Eve's golden delicious apple provided Adam with an insight into his need for clothing. I was therefore delighted to see a photograph of a Romanesque fresco of Adam and Eve, painted in the late 13th century in a chapel in Plaincourault, France. This depicts, between Adam and Eve, the snake wrapped, not in a fruit tree, but among what looks like a group of fly agarics. Eating such a mushroom would doubtless have altered Adam's view of the world. The Wassons, however, did their homework on this and learnt from an art historian that the 'mushroom tree' was nothing more than an impressionistically rendered Italian pine tree, typical of many early Christian paintings. Exit another conspiracy theory.

Rather more contentious than Eve's tempting fruit was the infamous book *The Sacred Mushroom and the Cross*, first published in 1970. Its author, John Allegro, a specialist in ancient Sumerian and Semitic languages, was part of an international team involved in piecing together, deciphering and publishing the Dead Sea Scroll fragments found at Qumran. Allegro's book argues that Christianity (and Judaism) is based on an ancient fertility cult centred on the fly agaric. Allegro interprets the Plaincourault fresco as a late recollection of this tradition and revels in the similarity between serpent and mushroom:

> *Both emerged from holes in the ground in a manner reminiscent of the erection of the sexually awakened penis, and both bore in their heads a fiery poison which the ancients believed could be transferred from one to the other.*

Sadly, my own Sunday School experiences were less exciting, perhaps because they predated Allegro's book. The book caused something of a fuss and resulted in a letter to *The Times* signed by no fewer than 15 university dons, declaring it to be an essay in fantasy rather than philology. From the mycological point of view there is no evidence for fly agaric's existence in the Middle East either today or in Biblical times.

Fly agaric has also been implicated as the drug that got the Vikings going; that is, made them go berserk, but most scholars feel that the behaviour of berserkers, including resistance to pain, does not fit the typical symptoms of those who have partaken of fly agaric.

I was reminded of the association between fly agaric and the wee folk when my daughter Bryony became too old to be a Brownie. A phone call from Brown Owl inviting my wife and me to witness our daughter 'flying up to guides' had my mind working overtime, but the reality was even better. Brown Owl emerged from a cupboard bearing a large, plastic, imitation fly agaric which she placed in the centre of the floor. As Bryony leapt over the mushroom she was accepted into the goblin six; a wonderful example of the ritual use of fly agaric in modern Britain. The year 2007 marked the centenary of the Scouting movement and part of the celebrations included a rally at the home of the first Scout camp, on Brownsea Island in Poole Harbour. The sandy soil of the island supports a thriving woodland community in which birch and pine predominate, along with large numbers of fly agarics!

In 1869 two German chemists analysed the chemical content of *Amanita muscaria*, a toadstool long reputed to be deadly poisonous. They discovered an alkaloid which they named muscarine, after the toadstool's scientific name. Muscarine has since been discovered in a number of poisonous fungi, the ingestion of which produces a range of symptoms, typified by profuse sweating, and which can prove fatal. Only later was it realised that the quantity of muscarine in fly agaric is insignificant and plays no part in the symptoms that are caused by ingesting the fungus.

In 1953 chemists reported finding another alkaloid in fly agaric. This was bufotenine, one of the chemicals found in the skin glands of toads (*Bufo* spp.). Given the historic use of toads as an ingredient in witches' flying ointments it was assumed that bufotenine in fly agaric was responsible for at least some of the symptoms of inebriation, and for a while there were attempts to rename the fungus the flying agaric. The presence of bufotenine in fly agaric was also a gift to those seeking the origins of the term toadstool (see page 11). Sadly for the conspiracy theorists it was shown, in the early 1960s, that there is no bufotenine in fly agaric, although it does occur in some related species.

By the mid-1960s the true nature of the chemicals that cause the symptoms of inebriation associated with eating fly agaric had been elucidated, but countless books continued to claim that 'poisoning' by fly agaric was due to muscarine or bufotenine. The new research came too late for the man condemned for the murder of a mushroom hunter in *The Documents in the Case* by Dorothy L. Sayers (see page 197). The principal chemical was first extracted by the Japanese, who named it ibotenic acid (from 'the long-nosed goblin mushroom with warts'), a chemical that readily breaks down, especially when the fungus is dried, to a much more potent chemical called muscimol. Muscimol is structurally similar to a chemical involved in our nervous system, helping to explain its likely mode of action. Most of the muscimol is not broken down by the kidneys and is rapidly passed into the urine, thus explaining the toxicity of mushroom eaters' urine.

The overall effects produced by consumption of fly agaric are extremely varied and this is likely to be due to a combination of factors. There is increasing evidence that the concentration of the toxic chemicals varies in different parts of the world. More importantly, there are big differences between fresh and dried samples, with gastrointestinal problems more likely after consumption of fresh mushrooms. Some hallucinations may occur, but the main effect is an alternation between deep sleep and manic behaviour, in total lasting for anything up to 9 hours.

Ibotenic acid and its derivatives have been found to stun flies, a property supporting the fly-killing reputation of the fungus. Ibotenic acid also acts as a flavour enhancer and was patented as such in 1969. Perhaps unsurprisingly it has not yet found its way into food products, but if it does they will no doubt be promoted as 'flying off the shelves'.

A Christmas Gift from Siberia

(For Tony and Patrick)

Santa lays his hand
on my head, and yours
a shaman
with gifts of healing
from worlds
the other side of the mushroom.
Rudolph carried him,
his nose as red as the scarlet fungus
with white spots
he shared with his master
to fly to the lands of wisdom.
Come into my house
where we huddle for warmth underground;
there's no need to knock
at my open door in the roof
where the smoke drifts out from the fire.
Welcome Santa
brave traveller'
healer.

Gillie Bolton
(First published in *The British Journal of General Practice*, December 2000)

Fungi on the Hoof

On 19th September 1991 a melting alpine glacier on the border between Italy and Austria disgorged a brown leathery body in its melt waters. The body was not that of any recent avalanche victim, for the iceman, or Otzi as he became known, turned out to date from the Neolithic period and had apparently been preserved in his icy tomb for over 5,000 years. Otzi had obviously been travelling and in addition to his copper axe he carried a wooden-framed backpack and an assortment of objects.

Among his possessions was a leather-belted pouch containing four blackened lumps and a collection of flints. The lumps turned out to be pieces of the fruitbody of a bracket fungus *Fomes fomentarius*, which has two common names: hoof fungus (describing its unusual shape) and tinder fungus. Analysis showed that the hard tissue of the fungus had been treated so as to loosen and soften it. That Otzi was carrying the means of starting a fire now seems without doubt as tinder fungus has been put to the same use for much of the past 5,000 years.

Before the introduction of matches, fire lighting was no easy task. The trick was to produce sparks either from the rotation of wood on wood or from flint struck on ironstone and later steel. Such sparks would not ignite pieces of wood, but were capable of causing dry tinder to smoulder and this (with the help of blowing) could produce a flame when applied to dried leaves and twigs. Tinder was almost exclusively made from fruitbodies of bracket fungi. The smouldering fruitbodies of puffballs were carried for the purpose of fire lighting, in this case eliminating the need for an initiating spark.

> *In divers parts of England where people dwell farre from neighbours they carry Fusse Balls [puffballs] kindled with fire which lasteth long, whereupon they were called Lucernarum Fungi.*
> John Gerard

Tinder was made not just from *Fomes fomentarius*, which in Britain is most commonly found on birch, but also *Phellinus igniarius*, the willow bracket, named after its most frequent British host. Young fruitbodies were soaked in water before being cut into thin strips, which were then beaten with a wooden mallet, rubbed and stretched to separate

the 'fibres'. The pieces then took on the appearance of old chamois leather, the resulting material being sold as red amadou. The addition of gunpowder or saltpetre (sodium nitrate) to produce what was called black amadou made an even more flammable material. The successful firing of a musket involved the hammer striking a flint and producing a spark, which ignited the amadou, which then set off the main charge.

In 1862 Mordecai Cooke (see page 182) wrote about the production of amadou and recorded that before the introduction of lucifers (matches), pipe smokers had needed to travel with a plentiful supply of amadou. The tinder fungus is most common in Scotland, where it was prepared for the British market, but considerable quantities were imported from mainland Europe. Other brackets occasionally used as tinder include birch bracket (*Piptoporus betulinus*), maze gill (*Datronia mollis*) and chicken of the woods (*Laetiporus sulphureus*).

Amadou was also used in medicine, both as a styptic and for cauterising wounds during surgery. Dentists used it to dry teeth before applying fillings (in the days before the blast of air), but one group of people still makes use of it. The art of fly fishing is full of mystery, nowhere more so than in the production and maintenance of the artificial flies cast on the water surface to lure unsuspecting fish. A good dry fly sits on the water surface, aided by a little oil and surface tension. Over time the oil wears off and the fly sinks, much to the consternation of the fisherperson. Help is at hand: the soggy fly is pressed in a fold of amadou, from which it emerges bone dry, ready to be re-oiled and sent on its way once more.

Otzi's association with fungi was not restricted to tinder in his fire-lighting kit. He also carried two pieces of birch bracket (*Piptoporus betulinus*), carefully held by a strap. As these were not protected in a bag it is unlikely that they too were used as tinder. Given the soft nature of his axe blade it is tempting to suggest that the birch bracket was carried as a means of sharpening it (stone would have been too harsh). An alternative name for *Piptoporus* is the razor strop fungus. Much more recently than 5,000 years ago it was used to strop (sharpen) razors by barbers. The fungus was sprinkled with sand or siliceous earth which would have lodged in the pores, suggesting that the fungus served the same job as the paper does in sandpaper.

Surprisingly, there is no archaeological evidence that the fibres from bracket fungi were used to make paper. Towards the end of the 20th century Miriam Rice, an American weaver and dyer, discovered that a wide range of common bracket fungi could be used to

FACING PAGE:
Hoof fungus – *Fomes fomentarius*

make paper in a manner similar to the making of paper from rags. Archaeological sites have, however, revealed another use for the fruitbodies of puffballs. In sites at Orkney (about 2,000 years old) and from Roman sites near Hadrian's Wall, large quantities of puffballs, mostly *Bovista nigrescens* were discovered. While these may have been involved in making and transporting fire it is now believed that they were an early form of insulation and draught excluder!

Puffballs have even been used by beekeepers wishing to gain access to their hives. In these cases smouldering giant puffballs (*Calvatia gigantea*) placed beneath the hives had an anaesthetic effect on the bees, possibly as a result of high levels of carbon dioxide. As late as the 19th century puffballs were put to a similar use as anaesthetics in hospitals. The charcoal-like fruitbodies of King Alfred's cakes (*Daldinia concentrica*) have been used for the same purpose and can also be used as a barbecue fuel.

While puffballs were used to calm bees, another fungus was implicated in killing flies. The common name for the infamous red and white spotted *Amanita muscaria* is fly agaric after its usage in medieval times as a fly killer. Strips of cloth (paper was too valuable) were soaked in milk in which chopped pieces of the fungus had been steeping. The strips were then hung from the ceiling where the fumes are said to have stupefied flies.

The making of paper from fungi may be a relatively recent craft, but in the 17th and 18th centuries certain fungal fruitbodies were used to manufacture ink. The two species most widely used were shaggy and common inkcaps (*Coprinus comatus* and *Coprinus atramentarius*), the fruitbodies of which rapidly disintegrate into a black inky fluid on maturity. This could be used straight or in a more concentrated form by boiling down. The addition of phenol helped to preserve the ink, although it still proved less permanent than more traditional inks made from plant sources. At one time it was suggested that fungal ink should be used for important legal documents and bank notes, as the absence of any spores in the ink would indicate a forgery. Today it is occasionally used by artists wishing to portray fungal portraits with fungal ink.

If fungal ink turned out to be a short-lived phenomenon the same cannot be said for the use of fungi as dyestuffs. The most important dyestuffs came not from the larger fungi but from lichens. Although lichens are dual organisms, the principal component of which is a fungus, and are now classified with the fungi, they are outside the scope of this book. For an interesting account of the use of lichens in the production of dyes, especially in Scotland and Wales, see the New Naturalist *Lichens* by Oliver Gilbert.

One non-lichenised fungus was formerly used in parts of southern Europe and also in the Canary Islands to produce a range of yellow (one possible origin of the term canary yellow) and brown dyes . Dye ball or devil's foot (*Pisolithus arhizus*) is related to the puffballs, but is more reminiscent of balls of horse dung. Its former scientific species name *tinctorius* (as in tincture) is found in plant species also used in dyestuffs, such as dyer's green weed *Genista tinctoria*. It is now so rare in Britain that it is on the Red Data List of Endangered Species.

Other fungi used as dyestuffs are mostly bracket fungi and their relatives. One of these is the shaggy bracket (*Inonotus hispidus*), a bracket whose upper surface resembles a door mat and is most frequent as a parasite on ash trees. It has been used to colour leather, silk and the wood used by cabinet-makers. The even odder-looking dyer's mazegill (*Phaeolus schweinitzii*) emerges like a cross between a cauliflower and a rusty spinning-top from the roots of conifers. It produces a range of colours from gold, through orange to brown. Natural dyes reigned supreme until 1856 when coal-tar dyes were invented, followed in the early 20th century by synthetic aniline dyes.

Along with papermaking and other crafts, the use of fungi as dyestuffs has recently enjoyed a revival and with this has come a search for novel fungal dyes. By using different chemical mordants, which both fix the dye and govern the colour obtained, a surprising number of agaric fungi has been shown to produce a wide range of colours. Among the best for producing reds and pinks are species of webcap (*Cortinarius*), while for orange try cep (*Boletus edulis*) as a change from eating it. Lemon–yellow originates from fly agaric (*Amanita muscaria*) and green from brown birch bolete (*Leccinum scabrum*).

While the exploitation of fungi for the manufacture of tinder, paper, ink or dyestuffs involves processing techniques and makes use of fungal fruitbodies, there are also examples of wood-rotting fungi in which the effect of the mycelium alters the appearance of the timber and in so doing imparts extra value to the wood. This is contrary to the popular belief that timber infected with a rotting fungus will have little or no value. The historic use of fungal-stained wood in Britain was centred on Kent and involved an ascomycete fungus known as the green elfcup. Despite the minute size of its fruitbodies, rarely more than 1 cm across, it has a very large scientific name, *Chlorociboria aeruginascens*. As it happens, it has recently changed both its common name (from green woodcup) and its scientific name (from *Chlorosplenium aeruginascens*). To add more confusion, in the eyes of many it is blue, not green! *Chlorociboria* grows as a saprophyte on fallen branches, most typically on oak and birch, but less commonly on other broadleaved trees. As the mycelium grows through the woody tissue it stains it a very conspicuous blue–green colour. The wood looks as if it has been artificially stained with a product such as Cuprinol.

Finding small pieces of blue–green-stained wood among the litter of a woodland floor is not difficult, but the fruitbodies are less common and are usually produced out of sight on the lower surface of the timber. They take the form of clusters of tiny, saucer-like objects between 2 and 10 mm across and attached to the wood by a short, delicate stalk. When fresh the discs are a vivid turquoise colour, but on drying they fade to a colour similar to that of the stained wood.

Formerly, this naturally green-stained wood was incorporated into Tunbridge ware, the term given to a wide range of wooden objects (sometimes known as treen) that were manufactured in and around the town of Tunbridge Wells in Kent. The trade appears to have started in the early 17th century to supply souvenirs for visitors to the newly discovered spa, later made famous by the royal patronage of Charles II. On visiting the spa in 1697, Celia Fiennes found a row of shops full of 'all sorts of curious woodenware, which this place is noted for'.

Early Tunbridge ware included both turned and marquetry work and was distinguished from treen made in other parts of England by its finer appearance and its use of many different, locally produced timbers to provide a pattern or picture without resorting to dyes, lacquer or paints. Included among the different timbers was the 'rare green': oak ('and certain other trees') stained by the green woodcup. In the early 19th century a form of decoration giving the appearance of a mosaic became synonymous with more valuable pieces of Tunbridge ware. The effect was achieved by gluing together thin strips of different coloured wood and then sawing across the block at different angles. Tunbridge ware was in decline by the end of the 19th century, and although it struggled on into the 20th century it was killed by competition from cheap, foreign, painted goods.

The demand for new patterned treen may be no more (although good pieces of Tunbridge ware fetch high prices), but there is still a healthy trade in turned wooden items both for display and use in the kitchen. Here, the pattern comes not from marquetry work but from the nature of the timber itself. To this end turners seek wood of intricate grain and also timber with a conspicuous pattern caused by wood-rotting fungi. Exposed stumps and cut ends of felled trunks often exhibit a jigsaw-like or 'world map' pattern of brown/black lines in the years following a tree's death. The colour is caused by melanin, which is produced at the boundaries of adjacent fungal individuals present in the wood. The unstained areas represent the mycelial territory of an individual. The patterns may represent several individuals of the same species or individuals of a number of different species.

Foremost among the timbers that may exhibit this type of patterning is beech. Spalted beech is the term given to beech wood displaying the dark boundary lines. Spalting usually occurs within 6–12 months of the felling or death of the tree. Over a longer time-scale the rotting action of the fungi makes the timber unsuitable, even for purely decorative items. Sound spalted beech wood with strong patterning is highly sought after and can fetch high prices. It makes wonderful chopping boards and is turned into plates and bowls.

A number of different fungal species can cause spalting in beech, including two ascomycete fungi. One of these is dead man's fingers (*Xlaria polymorpha*), the macabre fruitbodies of which are largely confined to beech stumps. The other is beech woodwart (*Hypoxylon fragiforme*), whose red/brown hemispherical lumps commonly festoon the bark of dead beech trees. The basidiomycete bracket *Trametes* (*Coriolus*) *versicolor* also causes spalting on beech, although this very common fungus grows on the dead wood of many different deciduous trees. In Britain it used to be called many zoned polypore, on account of its concentrically ringed fruitbody, but it has now become turkeytail, a name borrowed from our American cousins.

The beefsteak fungus (*Fistulina hepatica*), which produces a bloody-looking ox-tongue-shaped fruitbody, is also implicated in discolouring the heartwood of its host tree. In the early stages of infection the fungus causes a streaky brown effect. If the wood has not softened, the resultant 'brown oak' can fetch a good price. In a similar manner, 'calico wood' results from ash wood mottled by the influence of *Daldinia concentrica*, whose charcoal-like fruitbodies gave rise to its common name of King Alfred's cakes.

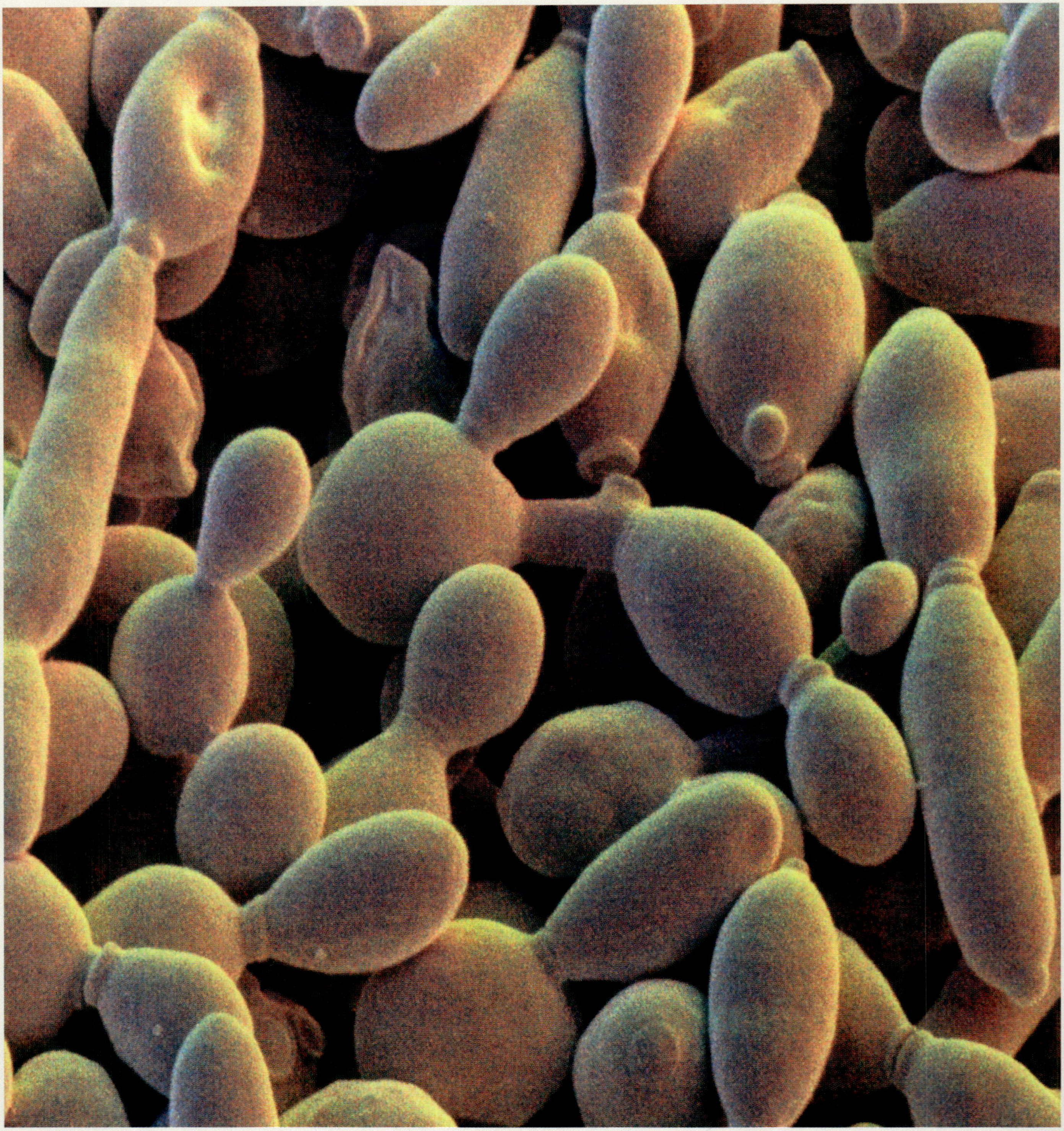

Love It or Hate It

The use of a range of fungal species, the most well known being brewer's yeast (*Saccharomyces cerivisiae*), in the production of various forms of alcohol dates back some 9,000 years. Similarly, the use of plants for their medicinal virtues has a long history. In the latter years of the 19th century German chemists extracted the efficacious chemicals from certain medicinal plants and began to synthesise similar chemicals in the laboratory. In 1899 salicylic acid from willow (the bark of which had long been used as a cure for headaches) was manufactured in the form of a less bitter-tasting molecule, what we now know as aspirin.

One of the pioneering 19th century German chemists was Baron von Liebig. He developed a process for transforming spent brewer's yeast (as it is called after it has been involved in the production of beer) along with remnants of the bitter hop extracts (added to improve the flavour and keeping quality of beer) into an edible, if not very appetising, paste known as yeast extract. Just 3 years after the launch of aspirin the Marmite Food Company initiated production of a product based on yeast extract in a disused malt house not far from the Bass Brewery in Burton-on-Trent. The recipe for Marmite includes the addition of salt, vegetable and spice extracts along with various synthetic B vitamins (thiamin, riboflavin, vitamin B_{12} and folic acid).

The distinctive tangy, salty taste of the resulting spread was not to everyone's liking, but by 1912 medical research had shown the importance of the B vitamins in preventing a range of illnesses and Marmite began to infiltrate our schools and hospitals. In 1922 the American firm of Fred Walker & Co. developed a rival yeast extract spread known as Vegemite. Produced in Australia and also sold in New Zealand, it aimed to satisfy demand for the Marmite taste among ex-patriots. During World War II Marmite was added to British soldiers' rations and was also part of the healthy eating campaign back home.

Marmite is a French word (pronounced mar-meet) for a stock pot or casserole dish, as pictured on its label. Prior to the switch to glass in the 1920s Marmite was sold in a small earthenware pot, mimicking a stock pot. Interestingly, both the Australian-

FACING PAGE:
Brewer's yeast – *Saccharomyces cerevisiae*, highly magnified

produced Vegemite (now part of Kraft Foods) and Marmite (now part of Unilever) manufactured in New Zealand contain added caramel and lack the real sharpness of the traditional British-produced Marmite. For this reason many a British visitor to family and friends in Australasia has acted as a courier for the real thing.

Marmite is still largely consumed only by the British (and their descendants) and it is widely believed that even in Britain people either love it or hate it – there is no room for any other view. The successful 1980s' 'My Mate' advertising campaign helped to boost sales and a 1998 survey found that 35% loved it, 38% hated it and this left 27% who had either never tried it or couldn't make up their minds. Aside from being spread very thinly on bread, toast or biscuits, it makes a nutritious hot beverage. A recent craze involves using the product to make pictures, otherwise known as Marmart. There are even unsubstantiated rumours of its use as an aid to better lovemaking, but these are beyond the scope of this book.

In 1994 a backpacker by the name of Paul Ridout was released after being kidnapped by Kashmiri separatists. On his return to Britain he is reputed to have eaten Marmite on toast to make up for what he had missed most during his captivity. Marmite has recently broken with tradition by being sold in new squeezey bottles. Traditionalists of a different kind, fans of Michael Bond, were not entirely happy to learn that Paddington Bear had switched from his beloved marmalade to having Marmite in his sandwiches. As I write this there is even a limited Valentine edition (in the traditional pot) sporting 'I LOVE YOU' and with 0.3% champagne, in addition to the usual ingredients. Fifty special pots have been created with an engraved silver lid. Marmite is moving with the times.

Mycelial Meals

As a student of Agricultural Botany in the 1960s I remember heated discussions that took place, mostly fuelled with nothing more dangerous than coffee, about the likely impact of the world population explosion. Foremost in people's minds at the time was the belief that as human numbers rocketed, the outcome would be a global shortage of protein. These predictions encouraged research into alternative protein sources that did not rely on the inefficient conversion of plant material into meat.

In 1967, around the time of my graduation, a filamentous microfungus (what the general public would call a mould) was collected from the soil of a field near Marlow in Buckinghamshire. It was a species of *Fusarium*, a fungus that is now included among the Hyphomycetes, within the Ascomycota (see page 25), the same group that contains species of *Penicillium*, from which antibiotics are obtained (see page 178). Species of *Fusarium* include those that cause dermatitis in whales, kill crocodiles, produce moulds on food left too long in refrigerators, rot bulbs, produce plant wilt diseases and, most intriguingly, provide food for a range of wood-boring insects known as ambrosia beetles.

Ambrosia beetles are close relatives of those that are responsible for spreading the spores of the fungus that causes Dutch elm disease (see page 111). Ambrosia beetles spread the spores of a different fungus which germinate in the tunnels made by the beetles in dead wood. The fungus is able to break down cellulose and lignin in the wood, materials that are indigestible to the beetles. The *Fusarium* mould produces a web of threads that lines the tunnel walls and this is eaten by the beetles and their larvae. This fungal ambrosia provides a rich source of protein, necessary for the growth of the developing beetles.

The *Fusarium* species collected in Marlow was originally identified as *Fusarium graminearum*, but was later correctly named *Fusarium venenatum*. Given that a related species provides a rich source of protein for beetles, could this one provide an alternative protein source for humans? In the West most consumers of mushrooms expect to eat the fruitbodies, but in the East certain foodstuffs have long been based on the mycelium rather than the fruitbody of a fungus. The problem with a diet that is low in animal protein but high in rice is that it deficient in lysine, an amino acid that is one of the

Quorn – fungal protein

essential building blocks of protein. Soya beans contain protein that is rich in lysine, but much of this is indigestible, even after cooking.

Tempeh, originating from Indonesia and now a staple food in many parts of south-east Asia, is made by inoculating soaked soya beans with a mould (typically *Rhizopus oligoosporus*). During production of the 'fermented' bean product, fungal enzymes from the *Rhizopus* mycelium convert soya protein to a form that is readily digestible by humans. The product, a mixture of beans and fungal mycelium, has a much firmer consistency than the better known tofu (a curdled soya bean product) and can be roasted, fried and readily frozen. It contains 40% protein, complete with all eight amino acids that are needed for protein synthesis.

When I gave up eating meat in 1980, neither tempeh nor tofu was widely available in Britain. The ubiquitous TVP (texturised vegetable protein) was like mince on a bad day and little favoured by non-meat eaters. The predicted world protein shortage had not come to pass, but the number of British vegetarians had increased so as to represent a significant proportion of the population. By this time production of what has been termed mycoprotein, from the mycelium of the *Fusarium* strain found 13 years earlier in Marlow, was in the final stages of development.

In 1985, following product approval by the Ministry of Agriculture, Fisheries and Food, Marlow Foods was formed to oversee the manufacture of a mycoprotein food product under the brand name of Quorn. The fungal mycelium is grown not on soya, but on food-grade glucose syrup, in a massive fermenter vessel. The rather phallic fermenter is 60 metres high and capable of producing 50,000 tonnes of protein a year. When it was transported to its current site and craned into an upright position it was described as the largest erection in the food industry's history.

The process is run in a continuous culture mode at a temperature of 30°C and a pH of 6. The constant addition of medium and growth of fungal hyphae is balanced by the withdrawal of the spent medium and harvesting of the mycelium. This is then processed by reducing the RNA content (which has a very bitter taste) and adding egg white and flavouring before it is cooked and shaped. The final product contains about 44% protein, similar to the amount in tempeh, and some two-thirds of the level in beef.

Mycoprotein contains only 13% fat (and no cholesterol), less than half the typical value found in beef. It also contains about 20% of dietary fibre, a component totally lacking in meat protein sources. Many Quorn products have a texture more akin to that of chicken breast and have appealed not just to vegetarians but also to the increasingly important health-food market.

In 1977 Rod Cooke forecast that 'yeast protein, termed single-cell protein, will become a major component of the diet of both man and his livestock'. As it turns out, the protein has come from a different fungus and it has taken nearer 30 years, but it was a very good prediction. Quorn-based foods, which now include over 70 different meat-free products from escallops and sausages to shepherd's pie, are now owned by Premier Foods. They are said to be eaten in more than 20% of the households in Britain, where they provide some 500,000 meals every day. With an annual retail value exceeding £100 million this places Quorn on a par with the value of mushroom sales in Britain.

لكنها الطف واغلظ واخشن واعرض وله قضيب طويل خشن مربع
ذا شجون كثيرة طول كل واحد ذراع وزهر صغير ارجواني واصله احمر
وينبت في الرياض الحسنة اصله ضمادا مع دقيق الشعير للحمرة واذا شرب
ادر العرق

اشبون له اوراق خشنة فيها بياض قليل تشبه اوراق خس الحمار لكنها
اصغر كثير وادهن وعليها شوك لطيف وبهذا الشوك تخشن الاوراق
وله قضبان كثيرة لطيفة مستديرة بها من الجانبين الاوراق كالاجنحة المتفرقة

Medicinal Moulds

For much of our history, mushrooms have been grouped with the plant kingdom. As a result, evidence of the medicinal use of fungi can be found in ancient herbals and writings about natural history. Such information covers a wide time-span and many different countries where different local names were used for the same species of fungus. The result of this is that care has to be taken with any interpretation of historical texts. In AD 77, the Roman writer Pliny the Elder (who died 2 years later in the eruption of Vesuvius) mentioned the use of mushrooms called suilli in his 37 volume *Historia Naturalis*:

> *Suilli are dried and hung up, being transfixed with a rush, as in those that come from Bithynia. These are good as a remedy in fluxes from the bowels which are called rheumatismsi, and for fleshy excrescences of the anus, which they diminish and in time remove: they remove freckles (letiginem) and blemishes on women's faces; a healing lotion is also made of them, as of lead for sore eyes; soaked in water they are applied as a salve to foul ulcers and eruptions of the head and to bites inflicted by dogs.*

In common with many plant remedies of the time, suilli acted as something of a cure-all. Suilli meant 'pig fungi' and it is fortunate that the meaning behind the old name is little changed to this day. In modern Italy they are referred to as porcini, meaning 'little pigs'. The old British name penny bun also relates to the bulbous shape of *Boletus edulis.* Today this is one of Europe's most sought-after edible mushrooms, but is no longer widely used for its medicinal properties.

Dioscorides, a famous Roman army doctor and contemporary of Pliny, gathered information about the medicinal properties of plants for his seminal work *De Materia Medica*, first published in AD 65. This includes one of the earliest references to 'agaricum', a bracket fungus believed to be *Fomitopsis officinalis*. This species is still found in southern Europe, typically on larch trees. It is a good example of a fungus that bears the specific name *officinalis*, an epithet that is frequent in the scientific name of medicinal plants such as dandelion (*Taraxacum officinalis*). The term indicates that it was sold from an 'office' or shop because it had a value.

FACING PAGE: Medieval Arabic herbal with text translated from that of Dioscorides

Confusingly, the modern word agaric is used as in the name fly agaric, for fungi with a central stem and umbrella-like cap, not in association with bracket fungi. It is evident that 'agaricum' was even more of a cure-all than suilli. Dioscorides lists a large number of complaints that were supposedly cured by the fungus. These included dysentery, fever, colic, kidney diseases, asthma, jaundice and other liver complaints. It was also said to be efficacious in the case of bruises and fractured limbs.

The teachings of Dioscorides held sway over much of Europe for at least 1,500 years, so it is not surprising to find that 'agaricum' remained something of a panacea and featured in Gerard's *Herball*, first published in 1597. Gerard included puffballs and Jew's ear (page 118) along with 'agaricum', but with the coming of a more experimental approach to science many of the earlier mushroom medications were dropped. The 1653 edition of Culpepper's *The Complete Herbal* did not mention any fungal species. Even so, 'agaricum', along with puffball and amadou, was listed in *Potter's New Cyclopedia of Botanical Drugs and Preparations* published in 1988.

The production and non-medicinal use of amadou is described on page 155. Tissue from the hard fruitbodies of two different species of bracket fungus was used: hoof fungus (*Fomes fomentarius*) and willow bracket (*Phellinus igniarius*). It was occasionally used as a surgical dressing and for wound staunching by surgeons, a use that continued into the 19th century. Unripe fruitbodies of giant puffball (*Calvatia gigantea*) were put to the same purpose. In parts of Scotland field mushrooms (*Agaricus campestris*) were sliced and put onto burns and scalds. Research into novel dressings for the treatment of leg ulcers and bed sores, using fungal mycelial filaments, is still in progress.

More intriguingly, amadou was occasionally used in parts of northern Europe as a form of moxa. This is more typically made from the wormwood plant (*Artemesia vulgaris*) and features in Chinese medicine. Small cones of moxa are burnt on the skin as a form of pain relief therapy, analogous to acupuncture. Culpepper included an account of this pain cure as used by Laplanders. Moxa cones smoulder, rather than burn with a flame, and the great plant explorer Joseph Hooker (later to become director of Kew Gardens) records a similar treatment, with a different fungus, when on his travels in Sikkim:

> *My servant having sprained his wrist by a fall, the Lepchas wanted to apply a moxa, which they do by lighting a piece of puffball, or Nepal paper that burns like tinder, laying it on the skin, and blowing until a large open sore is produced ...*
>
> J. D. Hooker, *Himalayan Journals*, 1854

Puffballs were more commonly used in Britain for their styptic properties, a fact mentioned by Gerard. He was not obviously enamoured by their culinary value as he records that 'Fusse-balls are no way eaten'. Fusse-ball was an old name for puffballs and one still encountered in some rural districts of England today. When still white and unripe, puffballs are now regularly eaten. The ripe fruitbodies were used for medicinal purposes, with the brown, powdery spore mass helping to staunch the flow of blood resulting from accident or surgery. The spores are a similar size to red blood cells and this may encourage speedier clotting. Puffballs are still used in this way today in both India and China. One 19th century account records that fumes from burning puffballs were used as an anaesthetic for surgery in a similar fashion to the use of burning puffballs by beekeepers (see page 158).

Gerard's 16th century record of medicinal fungi included Jew's ear fungus (*Auricularia auricula-judae*). Unlike 'agaricum', this had a much more limited medicinal use: it was believed to soothe sore throats. A liquid extract was prepared by either boiling the gelatinous fruitbodies in milk or steeping them in beer. The resulting fluid was then sipped slowly. It was probably not unlike some Chinese soups which utilise a related species of *Auricula*, known as wood ear. On account of its ability to absorb water it was also used as a topical astringent. Its medicinal use continued well into the 19th century as records show that Jew's ear was still sold at Covent Garden in 1860, a time when it was not considered a culinary species.

Many medicinal plants bear witness to their usefulness through their common names, such as selfheal (*Prunella vulgaris*) and woundwort (*Stachys* spp.), and there is one example of a common name for a British fungus that alludes to a medicinal use. *Daldinia concentrica* is now better known as King Alfred's cakes, but was previously known in certain parts of the country as cramp balls. The dark brown/black, hemispherical, charcoal-like lumps grow on ash trees. The cakes were placed between the sheets, but quite how, or if, they relieved the pain of cramp, remains a mystery! They are now better known as King Alfred's Cakes.

Another significant medicinal use of fungi mentioned in old herbals involves the oft-quoted use of moulds to prevent or cure infection resulting from open wounds. Mouldy cloth, mouldy leather and mouldy fruit or bread are all mentioned in a range of herbals. An old gypsy remedy for the treatment of boils involved the use of mouldy wheat straw. In Devon, Good Friday buns would be kept until they went mouldy and then used throughout the year as required. The story behind the introduction of penicillin, the first commercially produced antibiotic, is related on page 178. Scientific research at the end of the 20th century showed that moulds such as those associated with bread and fruit produce a substance called patulin. Although much less effective than penicillin it is a mild antibiotic, which adds substance to the historic use of moulds in medicine.

The *Herball* of Gerard mentions fungal aphrodisiacs, including the curiously named hart's truffle, in the genus *Elaphomyces*. Several species of *Elaphomyces* are found in Britain and, like the more famous culinary truffles, they produce subterranean fruitbodies. In the hart's truffle these are typically marble sized, purple–brown in colour and buried in the soil of coniferous woods. The aphrodisiac properties of the true truffles are discussed on page 87, but it is possible that this truffle owes its name to the belief that antlers were not the only body parts to be shed by forest deer. A later name for hart's truffle was Lycoperdon nuts. Earlier beliefs that *Elaphomyces* fruitbodies represented cast-off stag testicles or grew where deer had copulated were replaced by the doctrine of signatures. This was the tenet held by late medieval herbalists that a plant that resembled a body part or diseased organ would prove efficacious in curing the diseased part.

The position of underground hart's truffles is occasionally betrayed by the above-ground presence of *Cordyceps*, a fungus that parasitises the truffles. Of all the British species of *Cordyceps*, the best known is *Cordyceps militaris* (scarlet caterpillarclub), which emerges like a rough, orange matchstick; not from another fungus but from the moribund body of a caterpillar buried in the soil. The Chinese caterpillar fungus (*Cordyceps sinensis*) is very similar and has a long tradition as a 'herbal' medicine. An 18th century Western account of its use translated the Chinese name as winter worm/summer plant; the worm being the overwintering caterpillar and the plant being the club-like fungus (even the Chinese grouped many fungi with the plants). At the time it was said to cost more than four times its own weight in silver. By the middle of the 18th century the British mycologist Reverend Berkeley had correctly identified the 'plant' portion as being of fungal origin.

Although no longer priced with reference to silver, the Chinese caterpillar fungus is not common and is still highly prized and priced accordingly. High in the mountains of Sichuan Province, where there is still snow in June, the orange clubs are easier to spot as they grow through the snow. The fungus, including the larval body, is washed and dried, ready for use. One way is to add boiling water and make a tea from the dried material, another is to presoak it in alcohol before drinking the resultant liquor. Traditional methods involve cooking and eating a duck stuffed with the fungus/caterpillar.

The Chinese caterpillar fungus is looked on as a tonic and is used by those recovering from serious illness. The remedy came to the attention of the Western press when investigating the unexpected success of some Chinese athletes in the Olympic Games of the 1990s. *Cordyceps* and its constituent compound 'cordycepin' were not on the list of banned substances, but are thought to be especially beneficial in improving stamina for participants in long-distance events. As with a host of other Chinese herbal remedies the supposed therapeutic effects of *Cordyceps* are now being closely analysed by Western pharmaceutical firms.

Just as the Olympics highlighted one Eastern medicinal use of a fungus in the 1990s, a famous book published in 1968 was to generate interest in the use of fungal extracts in the fight against cancer. Aleksandr Solzhenitsyn's *The Cancer Ward* focused Western eyes on the Russian practice of drinking a tea made from the woody bracket fruitbody of the birch conk (*Inonotus obliquus*). Not infrequent in Scotland, the fungus causes black swellings (conks) which erupt through the bark of infected birch trees. That a tumour-like swelling should be used as an anticancer treatment has all the hallmarks of the ancient doctrine of signatures. Coupled with a general scepticism originally shown by Western scientists to work emanating from behind the Iron Curtain, it is not surprising that such claims were initially dismissed as old folk remedies.

In the ensuing years Western researchers have investigated a number of chemicals found in the fungal conk. The principal component, known as inotodiol, has been shown to have antitumour properties. It also has antiviral properties and shows promise in the fight against many forms of the influenza virus and HIV infection.

The chemicals associated with the birch conk are not the only ones to have caught the interest of big pharmaceutical companies in the past 50 years. For thousands of years Ling Zhi has been a revered Chinese herbal remedy, which was once rated above ginseng. In Japan, where it is called Reishi, it has long been valued for its medicinal properties and was formerly reserved for use by emperors and royalty. Ling Zhi and Reishi are different names for the same fungus, *Ganoderma lucidum*, yet another woody bracket fungus. In Britain it is known as the lacquered bracket as its kidney-shaped fruitbodies look as if they have been varnished. In the wild the bracket grows from the roots of trees (not on the trunks) and occasionally occurs on the apex of a long, dark woody 'stem'. This is the form most sought after in China, where the whole fruitbody is sold, along with extracts in tablets and as an alcoholic drink. *Ganoderma* is now cultivated on sections of 30-year-old Japanese oak that have been buried in soil.

In a manner similar to the early Western use of 'agaricum', the use of *Ganoderma* in the Far East has been implicated in the curing of a huge range of illnesses including various cancers, heart disease, hepatitis and bronchitis. Traditionally, it was an elixir of long life. The fungus contains a number of unusual chemicals and many of these are currently being screened to assess their therapeutic potential.

Sales of *Ganoderma*-based products have yet to take off in Britain, but one oriental mushroom, shiitake (*Lentinula edodes*), has seen a huge increase in sales, especially of the fresh fruitbodies. The firm texture and unique flavour of shiitake have long been valued in oriental cooking, but the introduction of novel techniques allowing the fungus to be cultivated in Britain (see page 81) has spearheaded its increasing popularity as a food. Shiitake may be more than a food as it contains some unusual chemicals, notably lentinanin, which has been shown to have antiviral and antitumour activity.

The fungal problems associated with diet in earlier times are discussed on page 133 with reference to ergot (*Claviceps purpurea*), a fungus that parasitises the flowers of members of the grass family including many cereal crops. Hundreds of years before scientists showed the link between the black, banana-shaped outgrowths (sclerotia or 'ergots') from the ears of cereal and the problems caused by eating ergot-contaminated flour, midwives throughout Europe had discovered a medicinal use for the fungus.

The earliest written record of the obstetric use of decoctions made by boiling ergot sclerotia in water dates from the late 16th century. By the 18th century ergot was being used in France, Germany and Italy. Records from North America go back to the mid-1700s and in 1808 an American journal published an account of the use of ergot for quickening childbirth. In the early 19th century the drug was part of pharmacopoeias in both America and Britain. Ergot decoctions did not simply ease and quicken labour by stimulating muscle contractions, they also reduced bleeding by promoting rapid expulsion of the afterbirth; a major cause of death following childbirth.

The first medicinal use of ergot pre-dates knowledge of the chemical cocktail which is now known to be contained within the sclerotium. The most likely explanation of the discovery of ergot's medicinal use lies with the fact that in large doses ergot is an abortificant, inducing early, violent uterine contractions. A means of ending foetal life became (in a lower dose) one of saving the mother's life. The precise mix of chemicals contained in the 'ergots' has taken over a century to unravel. At least a dozen alkaloids have been isolated, including ergotamine in 1918 and ergometrine (known as ergonovine in America) in 1935.

Ergometrine maleate has been extensively used in obstetrics and, although now often replaced by more modern drugs, including oxytoxin, many female readers of this account will have vivid memories of the injection given shortly after childbirth. Few will realise that this was just a modern way of utilising ergot's beneficial effects. Ergotamine tartrate, which induces dilatation of peripheral blood vessels, has been widely used to alleviate the symptoms of migraine.

The active ingredients of ergot proved difficult to synthesise and for many years the pharmaceutical industry relied on ergot grown on cereal crops in parts of Russia and Spain. Supplies are now obtained from laboratory-grown cultures as, unusually for a parasite, ergot can be grown as a saprophyte on a culture medium.

Between the two World Wars ergot's chemical factory caught the attention of many of the world's big pharmaceutical companies on the lookout for novel medicinal drugs. Foremost among these was the Swiss firm of Sandoz Pharmaceuticals (now Novartis) where, in the 1930s, Albert Hofmann was investigating derivatives of ergot alkaloids and related compounds. In 1938 he produced the 25th derivative of lysergic acid, codenamed LSD-25, but it was not until 5 years later that its effects were discovered.

The impact of this discovery on counter-culture and literature is covered elsewhere in this book (see pages 141 and 198), but what is often forgotten is the part played by LSD as a potential aid to psychiatrists in the treatment of mental illnesses during the 1950s and early 1960s. After LSD-25 was patented it was made available to the medical world. As a therapeutic tool combined with more conventional counselling it appeared to provide a rapid means of exposing long-repressed memories and emotions in patients with mental health problems and thus to provide a means to a speedier recovery.

Unfortunately for those interested in the clinical use of LSD for psychotherapy research, the drug came to the attention of members of the CIA who were searching for a mind-control drug that could be of use in the interrogation of spies. Experimentation that began within the military and with compliant individuals, spread to jails, college dormitories and brothels, where the antics of unsuspecting clients were observed by CIA officials. When several people died or suffered severe mental damage as a result of this clandestine research and the world's media got hold of the story, more legitimate research programmes involving LSD were starved of funding. With the rise of the drug as part of 1960s' culture, Sandoz stopped manufacturing it. Soon after this, legislation outlawing LSD followed in both America and Britain.

At the same time that the use of ergot was being accepted into mainstream medicine in the early decades of the 19th century, a respected German physician by the name of Samuel Hahnemann introduced a new approach to medicine in the form of homoeopathy. In contrast to normal allopathic medical treatments, which are given in an attempt to suppress the symptoms of disease, Hahnemann's approach was to treat with something that produces (in a large dose when given to a healthy patient) an effect similar to the symptoms. For example, an extract of deadly nightshade (*Atropa belladonna*) induces a range of symptoms in a healthy person that is remarkably similar to the symptoms shown by a patient suffering from scarlet fever. Homoeopaths may choose to treat patients suffering from scarlet fever with a very dilute extract of deadly nightshade. A very dilute solution may contain no chemicals from the initial extract, one reason why many scientists attack the concept of homoeopathy as being without a scientific basis.

Despite the antipathy to homoeopathy shown by the majority of the medical profession a considerable proportion of the British public use homoeopathic remedies for a wide range of conditions. Most of the established remedies are, like deadly nightshade, of plant origin and derive their names, as in the case of Belladona, from the plant's scientific name. Some are derived from naturally occurring chemicals, others from animal products and a few from the fungal kingdom.

None of the most commonly used homoeopathic remedies of fungal origin is easily identifiable from the remedy name. Secale cornutum is the homoeopathic remedy made from ergot (*Secale* is the scientific first name for rye, the cereal most affected by ergot), and most confusingly of all Agaricus is not prepared from 'agaricum' (see page 170) or from *Agaricus* (a mushroom), but from *Amanita muscaria* (fly agaric), which in the time of Hahnemann was classified under *Agaricus*.

Given the symptoms shown by those suffering from ergotism (see page 133) it should be of no surprise to learn that Secale is used homoeopathically in the treatment of convulsions, neurological disorders and heavy periods. The effects of eating fly agaric are described in Chapter Thirty one and explain the homoeopathic use of Agaricus in treating visual anomalies, fear and stammering.

Of all the fungal products in medicine, the story of the introduction of the first antibiotic eclipses all others by nature of its importance in the history of medicine. As with many important discoveries the story has lost a little in the telling. The initial discovery by Dr Alexander Fleming, working at St Mary's Hospital in London in 1928, is well recorded. Fleming had been studying the growth of bacterial colonies cultured in Petri dishes when he noticed that in one dish the bacterial colony had been killed off in the presence of a contaminant mould that had 'spoilt' the experiment. Legend has it that the mould spore had blown in through an open window, but this is very unlikely. The mould was identified as a species of *Penicillium*, from where Fleming took the name penicillin for a chemical compound from the mould that had killed the bacteria in his Petri dish.

Penicillin mould on an orange

In the minds of many there is but a small jump from its initial accidental discovery to the introduction of penicillin as a life-saving drug towards the end of World War II and the subsequent knighthood awarded to Fleming for services to medicine. The real story is what went on *after* 1928. Among the questions requiring answers were: what types of bacteria were killed by penicillin; would the chemical work in the body as well as in a Petri dish; how stable was the drug; were there any side-effects from penicillin or other drugs in the fungal brew; how could the concentration of penicillin be increased to facilitate industrial production; and what was the molecular structure of penicillin?

Fleming and a small team at St Mary's Hospital answered some of these questions, but were unable to obtain sufficient quantities of suitably pure penicillin to enable clinical testing on animals. Fleming discontinued his studies on penicillin and the discovery lay largely dormant for almost a decade. Then in 1938 Drs Howard Florey and Ernst Chain began a systematic study at Oxford University into naturally produced antibacterial substances. Among these was penicillin.

Florey and Chain were able to obtain a subculture of the original *Penicillium* mould from St Mary's Hospital. This was fortunate as Fleming had assumed that the mould species was *Penicillium rubrum*, but it had been incorrectly identified and was in fact *Penicillium notatum* (we now know that *rubrum* produces very little penicillin). When Fleming visited the team at Oxford he is reputed to have quipped, 'I understand you have been working with *my* mould', a comment that did not go down well with Florey and Chain, who later made it clear that they felt Fleming got far more credit for penicillin than he deserved.

Chain managed to produce a pure sample of penicillin using the then relatively new technique of freeze-drying. Not only did the sample kill bacteria in culture, it did not cause side-effects when Florey injected some into animals. In 1940 penicillin was shown to cure mice suffering from a *Streptococcus* bacterial infection. Just 6 months later an Oxford policeman dying of blood poisoning caused by *Staphylococcus aureus* was treated with the drug, resulting in a dramatic improvement in his condition. Tragically, however, supplies ran out and the bacterium killed him.

What was needed was a way of producing large amounts of pure penicillin in a stable form, but British industry was too tied up with the war effort at this time. Florey moved to Illinois where a laboratory was looking for uses for a local agricultural waste product: corn steep liquor, left over after starch had been extracted from maize. This medium proved so good at growing the mould that the output of penicillin was quickly increased some 20-fold. Staff from the laboratory also started collecting a range of *Penicillium* moulds and some of these, including *Penicillium chrysogenum* from a rotting cantaloupe melon, proved unusually rich in penicillin. By 1943 the yield was 500 times greater than from the Fleming's original experiments.

The knowledge that penicillin could save the lives of many soldiers meant that much of the work was covered by the Official Secrets Act and in America the work was granted a higher priority than any military item with the exception of the atomic bomb. Many different firms put aside their rivalry as part of the war effort but when, later, companies learnt to synthesise penicillin derivatives, a long-running battle ensued over patent rights. In 1945 Fleming, Florey and Chain won the Nobel Prize for Medicine.

After the war the search for new moulds continued. From a *Cephalosporium* mould (it has since had its name changed to *Acremonium chrysogenum*) collected near a sewage pipe on the coast of Sardinia came the cephalosporins, antibiotics that work in a manner similar to the penicillins. By 1997 worldwide sales of antibiotics were worth £6,000 million. A different species of *Penicillium*, *P. griseofulvum*, yielded griseofulvin, a chemical that kills not bacteria but other fungi; this has proved efficacious against fungi that cause human ailments such as ringworm and thrush.

A different group of chemicals, known as cyclosporins, were obtained from a range of soil-inhabiting fungi including *Tolypocladium inflatum*. These chemicals suppress the body's immune system and are behind the increased success rate of organ transplants previously rejected by the recipient's immune system. Rheumatoid arthritis and some forms of inflammatory bowel disease, which are autoimmune system disorders, are also treated with cyclosporins.

More recently a group of drugs known as statins has received huge publicity. Statins work by inhibiting cholesterol synthesis and reduce the risk of disease caused by high cholesterol levels. These are produced, or partly synthesised, from a range of moulds and yeast-like fungi. Increasingly, statins are being totally synthesised, but as with many antibiotics the original drugs were derived from fungi.

Some fungi cause disease and discomfort, but products from others have proved highly efficacious and are important member of the arsenal of drugs used in modern medicine.

M.C.C.

The man who was to become Britain's first professional mycologist, Mordecai Cubitt Cooke, was born in Norfolk in 1825 into a deeply religious family of Baptists who also had great faith in education. To this end he was sent to Ilford, at the age of 10, to continue his schooling with an uncle, James Cubitt, a highly educated Baptist minister. Years later, Mordecai wrote:

> *My uncle grounded me well in the rudiments of Latin, Greek, algebra etc. ... and sent me with instructions to make collections of the plants and flowers that grew by the wayside, and to classify and name them afterwards with such assistance as I could get from his little botanical library.*

At 15 his education ceased and he spent 5 years as clerk to a drapery business in Norwich, where as a strict teetotaller he joined both a temperance band and the local choral society. In 1845 he moved to London and a year later, when he was 21, married Sophia Biggs, a woman of 23 with an illegitimate 2-year-old daughter named Annie. In 1851 Mordecai presumably passed Annie off as his own child to procure his next job as a trainee teacher at the Holy Trinity School in Lambeth, where he worked for 9 years. Here he first ventured into writing, with an article on the teaching of 'natural history' in *The School and the Teacher*. He also made use of the Natural History Museum, which opened to the public in 1857. Cooke's interest in museums led him to a part-time directorship of the Scholastic Museum, one of many museums set up in the second half of the 19th century to inform people about the wonders of science.

On a visit to his native Norfolk, 'to give a gossiping lecture to the rustics in the schoolroom', he met the local squire, Richard Ward, whose hobby was edible fungi. Many of Ward's finds had been identified by the Reverend Berkeley (often regarded as the father of British mycology) and Ward collected specimens for the museum at Kew Gardens, then under the directorship of Joseph Hooker. Cooke later wrote that his meeting with Ward inspired him to turn his attention to 'toad-stools' and especially the edible species which he had previously been taught to regard as 'rank p'isen'. He later recorded; 'Since that eventful evening I have never abandoned the pursuit and it has been my solace'.

Given this, it is perhaps not surprising that one section of Cooke's first published book *The Seven Sisters of Sleep* ('a popular history of the seven prevailing narcotics in the world') concerned the hallucinogenic properties of the fly agaric toadstool. His chapter on tobacco was rather light hearted, perhaps a result of his own addiction to the weed. It was not his smoking that lost him his teaching job, but the fact that he was teaching too much science. When in 1860 the new incumbent at the parish began interfering with the school, Cooke, in his typically blunt manner, 'recommended him to attend to his duties at the Church and leave me to do my duties at the Schools. This, of course, led to my being advised to resign which I did forthwith'.

His next full-time job was working with the collections and displays of 'vegetable products' in the India Museum in Whitehall, where he stayed for 18 years. In 1867, Mordecai was promoted and given a better salary which, together with money that came to him following his father's death in 1869, allowed him to buy his own house. By this time his family had expanded, although Mordecai's first child did not arrive until he had been married to Sophia for over 16 years. Harry Linnaeus was born in 1862, and Ada, Willie and Ernest followed at 2-yearly intervals. As it happened, the woman who bore his four children was not Mordecai's wife Sophia, but his stepdaughter Annie, who was 17 when Harry was born.

Quite how the aspiring Mordecai got away with this amazing arrangement is not known, but family life became even more complicated when in 1870, just as the family moved to their new home, Annie was pregnant again, not by Mordecai but by a 24-year-old relative (John Cubitt) who had been staying with the Cookes! She and John subsequently married and moved to shared lodgings, before the birth of Mabel. At this point Sophia resumed her role as 'mother' to the remaining four children in Cooke's house.

Mordecai's first book exclusively about fungi was *Plain and Easy Account of British Fungi*. At the time there were hardly any British books on fungi aimed at the general public. It was a very readable book and remained in print for 36 years. At the foot of page 4 he instructs amateurs that pronunciation of the g in fungus is hard, but in fungi the g should be soft. His Latin education also lay behind his scorn of those who talked about funguses rather than fungi. Mordecai and his brother Ebenezer produced the colour illustrations for his book.

During his 18 years at the India Museum Mordecai wrote countless articles, and at least a dozen books, many on fungi, but others on botany, ferns and reptiles. As a member of various field clubs he enjoyed escaping from London, and the confines of his job and family. The latter was still growing, as was Annie, whose sixth child born in 1875 was probably Mordecai's, for Annie was breaking up with John and later moved back in with the Cookes, bringing Mabel and the new baby, Frank, with her! When Herbert was born in 1879, Mordecai was 54 and his wife Sophia 56, beyond the age of childbearing. Still, Mordecai appears to have kept his unusual family life apart from his work, publishers and the world of mycology. Sophia must have assumed the role of grandmother (which she was) and Annie that of Mordecai's wife.

Mordecai became a leading light of the Woolhope Naturalist's Field Club, whose members were mostly clergymen and professional men from the new middle class. Set up to further practical study of natural history in the county of Herefordshire, it included October field meetings such as the 1868 'Foray amongst the Funguses' followed by dinner at the Mitre Hotel. Here Mordecai rubbed shoulders with eminent mycologists whose antics were recorded in the cartoon-like illustrations of Worthington Smith. Cooke was also an active member of the Royal Horticultural Society and the Quekett Microscopical Club. Dinners held by the latter club were frequently attended by Cooke singing his own witty verses, many bearing reference to the joys of alcohol and proving that he had relinquished his earlier sobriety.

In 1880, following dispersal of the plant collection from the India Museum to Kew Gardens and the gift of Berkeley's collection of 20,000 fungal specimens, Mordecai was appointed to work on the collections for 3 days a week. So began his link with Kew that was to continue until his retirement in 1892 at the age of 67. Cooke was Britain's first professional mycologist. One of Cooke's greatest achievements at this time was to produce 1,200 plates, arranged in eight volumes, of *Illustrations of British Fungi*. Today the collection at Kew has over 600,000 specimens; the most important such collection in the world. Sadly Cooke's bluntness and outspokenness did not enamour him to William Thistleton-Dyer, the garden's Assistant Director who took over the directorship on Hooker's retirement in 1885.

On his own retirement, Cooke's youngest child Leila, born in 1882, was just 10. This led him to sell his herbarium collection, containing 40,000 specimens of fungi, to Kew. By 1890 Annie had moved out again and this time she did not come back. Mordecai continued to be active in mycology, especially on field meetings. By this time the Yorkshire

Naturalist's Union had taken over the mantle of the Woolhope Club, as the organiser of fungal forays. In 1895 Cooke was present, along with George Massee, his successor at Kew, when the idea of setting up a national society was mooted. The following year saw the inauguration of the British Mycological Society. The BMS is still going strong and continues to welcome amateur mycologists in addition to its professional members.

Cooke continued to publish articles and books. His 1894 *Edible and Poisonous Mushrooms: What to Eat and What to Avoid* included English names for all 48 species. In common with writers of books about fungi in the 20th and 21st centuries it is apparent that he made up some of the English names! In 1897 his long-suffering wife Sophia died and shortly afterwards Mordecai and Leila moved to a smaller house, where she took over the role of caring for him. In 1902 the Royal Horticultural Society awarded Cooke its Victoria Medal of Honour and the following year he was presented with the Linnaean Society's Gold Medal. In his old age, the *Morning Post* ran an article about him, to celebrate his 87th birthday.

The article had an unfortunate consequence. Dr John Ramsbottom (author, some 40 years later, of the New Naturalist *Mushrooms and Toadstools*) took the article to be an obituary and passed the news to staff at Kew Gardens. There followed obituaries of Cooke in the *Kew Bulletin*, *The Times* and other national papers. A few days later Cooke wrote:

> *My dear Sir, Permit me to warn you against falling into the error of the Kew Bulletin, The Times, D.T. and some others of announcing my death, which has not yet taken place – nor have I taken to my bed except at the orthodox sleeping hours* 10.30 *p.m. to* 8.30 *a.m. daily. My doctor visits me occasionally, inspects my tongue, feels my pulse, and nods his head, but has not yet declared me to be dead.*

Mordecai lived on for another 2 years; he was in his 90th year and the Great War had started. He outlived his friends and colleagues, but one final enigma was to die with him. He had never liked the name Mordecai (he was a lapsed Baptist, never a Jew), but it had been in the family from as early as the 17th century. To his family he was known as MC, and he did not pass on the name to any of his many children, despite the family belief that if this was not done the Cooke family would die out. Two of his sons died from falls before they married, Frank was not sired by Mordecai and died unmarried, leaving only Willie of his sons. Willie did marry and had a child, a daughter, so the prophecy came true and with the death of the enigmatic Mordecai, the Cooke family also died.

Boletes to Bunnies

For millions of people, the name Beatrix Potter is inseparable from her delightful books epitomised by *The Tale of Peter Rabbit*. Children and adults in many different countries still enjoy her wonderful illustrations, and in places such as Japan, her books are set texts for those learning English. The recent *Miss Potter* film highlighted her publishing record, relationships and the wonderful landscapes of the Lake District in which she made her home, but ignored a major theme in Beatrix's early life: her interest in fungi.

We can find a clue to her mycological knowledge in *The Fairy Caravan*, in which she describes Paddy Pig's ill-health following the consumption of toadstool tartlets, including symptoms of odd behaviour and the use of Rue to cure him. In the poem *The Toad's Tea Party* her illustration shows seven toads seated on toadstools enjoying a meal including 'pats of witches' butter', a common name for the black, jelly-like fungus *Exidia glandulosa*. Fame, marriage and life in the Lake District came late to Beatrix, but it was while she was on family holidays as a younger woman in Scotland that she developed a passion for what she called funguses.

From the time when Helen Beatrix Potter was a small girl (she was born in 1866), her parents had taken the family to spend the summer in Perthshire, renting houses in the area around Dunkeld. When Beatrix was in her twenties she painted a series of watercolours of fungi, many of which she found in the Perthshire countryside. Her mentor for the scientific names on her paintings came from a most unlikely source, their shy postman, Charles McIntosh, also known as the 'Perthshire Naturalist'. With Charles' encouragement and the help of a microscope, Beatrix pursued her interest.

Many of her beautiful watercolour paintings are preserved in the Armitt Library in Ambleside. Included in her illustrations were the rare pink waxcap (*Hygrocybe calyptriformis*) (see page 95), green elfcup (*Chlorociboria aeruginascens*) (see page 159) and the rarely recorded old man of the woods (*Strobilomyces strobilaceus*). These pictures, among others, were reproduced in Findlay's *Wayside and Woodland Fungi*, published by Frederick Warne, the publisher responsible for all the Peter Rabbit books, in 1967.

FACING PAGE: The Toad's Tea Party painted by Potter for the unpublished *Book of Rhymes*

In 1896, when Beatrix was 30, her distinguished uncle, Sir Harry Roscoe, procured an introduction to Kew Garden's professional mycologist, George Massee. She met Massee and the Kew director, William Thistleton-Dyer. At the time little was known about the germination of fungal spores and the early growth of fungus mycelium. Beatrix had not only managed to culture germinating fungal spores but also produced very accurate illustrations of this stage in the life cycle of fungi. This was at a time when such work had not been achieved in Britain by professional mycologists. Beatrix later recorded in her journal that the snobbish Thistleton-Dyer had informed her that he hadn't the time to look at her drawings, although he did find time to write to Beatrix's uncle about the time-wasting problem of meddling amateurs.

Sir Harry Roscoe was so annoyed at the attitude shown by Kew's director that he helped Beatrix in the preparation of a formal scientific paper for the Linnaean Society. The following April (perhaps appropriately it was 1st April 1897), George Massee read a paper to the meeting of the Linnaean Society, 'On the germination of the spores of *Agaricaceae*', by Helen B. Potter. At the time women were not allowed to present papers or even attend the meeting! There was little reaction to the paper and this probably marked a turning point in the life of Beatrix. Rabbits, rather than mushrooms, were to make her famous.

Poetry, Prose, Pop and Pictures

It is tempting to seek a correlation between the tone of a nation's literary (and visual) depiction of mushrooms and toadstools and its people's enthusiasm for fungi. But in which direction is the relationship? Some authors have argued that a country's attitude towards mushrooms has been moulded by the pen of its writers. The typically mycophobic (mushroom-hating) attitude historically shown by peoples of Anglo-Saxon descent, spearheaded by the British and their descendants in the United States, Canada and Australia, is certainly mirrored in their literature. It is more likely that these writings are the *result* of cultural bias rather than its *cause*. As Professor Denis Benjamin states, 'It is unlikely that the mass of humanity was greatly affected by much of this early writing, because most had no access to it, nor could they read'.

In the British context, the wisdom of hindsight reveals that many damning passages written about fungi by herbalists, poets and others resulted from an unquestioning copying from earlier works, compounded by a total lack of scientific knowledge about the group. On page 170 the work of Dioscorides, a contemporary of Pliny, is discussed with reference to the medicinal properties of fungi. From the 15th to the early 17th centuries the chief preoccupation of many herbalists was the elucidation of the work of Dioscorides, written some 1,500 years earlier.

> *Fungi ben mussherons … There be two manner of them; one manner is deedly and sleeth them that eateth of them and be called tode stooles, and the other dooth not. They that be not deedly have a grosse gleymy moisture that is dysobedyent to nature and dygestyon and be peryllous and dredfull to eate & therefore it is good to eschew them all.*
>
> (The grete herbal whiche giveth parfyt knowledge and understanding of all manner of herbes and there gracious vertues, 1526)

Despite the rather vain title, this work was a compilation of several 15th century works from mainland Europe and the woodcuts came from a German herbal of 1485. It is interesting to note that Hieronymus Braunschweig, who used the same illustrations in a

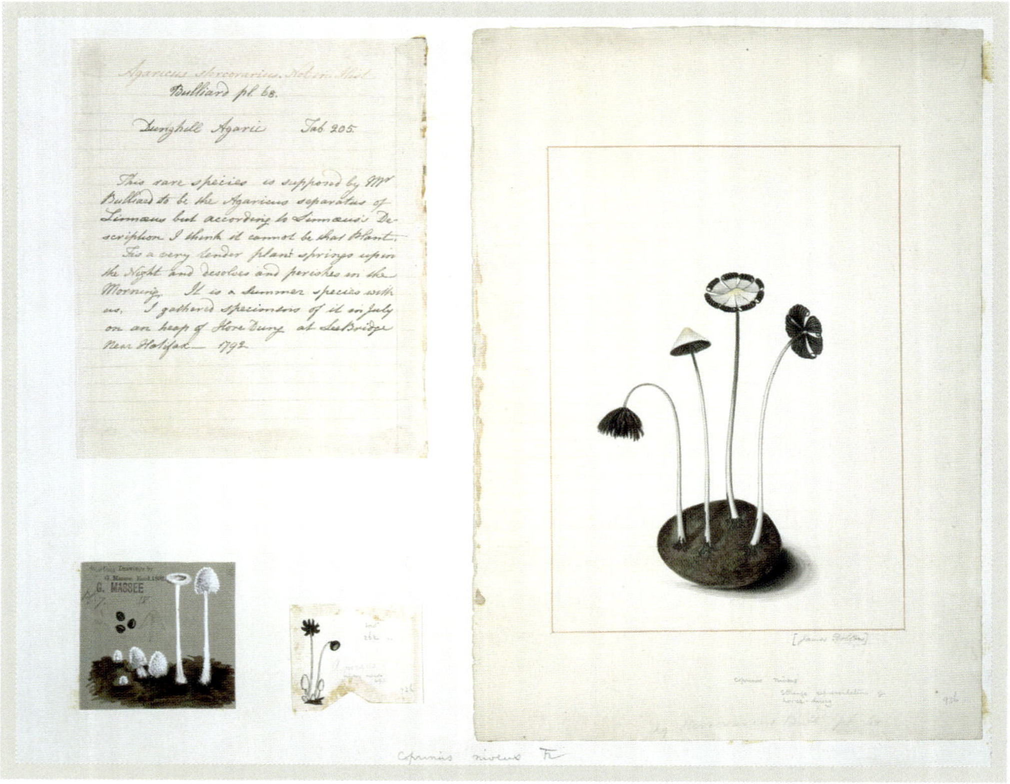

Agaricus slercorarius, from Fungi Illustrations (1792) by James Bolton

book of his, informed readers: 'for the figures are nothing more than a feast for the eyes, and for the information of those who cannot read or write'.

The illustrations that accompanied the texts by the Italian herbalist Pierandrea Mattioli were much more accurate and one of these, in his 1560 publication, *Commentari*, includes a plate labelled 'fungi'. The snail in the foreground exemplifies the contemporary slimy image of fungi, while the inclusion of a snake stresses the supposedly venomous nature of mushrooms. Another 16th century writer declared that snails crept out of their shells, turned into toads, and then feeling the need of something to sit upon, fashioned toadstools for themselves. From medieval times, mushrooms, toads, snails and snakes were all regarded as dangerous and evil, not least because of their supposed association with witches, in league with the devil. Pictures depicting hell were liberally strewn with toads, snakes and mushrooms.

One of the best known English botanical books, John Gerard's *The Herball* (first edition 1597) was mostly taken (without acknowledgement) from the 1554 work of Rembert Dodoens.

> *Few mushrooms are good to be eaten and most do suffocate and strangle the eater. Thereof I give my advice unto those that love such strange and new fangles meates to be beware licking the honey among the thorns lest the sweetness of one do not countervaile the sharpness and pricking of the other.*
>
> *Many that do have plenty of both (fish and birds) do hunger after the earth's excrescence's called mushrooms, whereof some are venomous, others not so noisome, and neither of them very wholesome meat. Whereof for the avoiding of the venomous qualities of the one, and the other which is less venomous may be discovered, I have thought good to set forth their pictures with their names and places of growth.*

Only 18 of the 2,000 illustrations were original and included a woodcut entitled 'the breede of Barnakles', illustrating the ancient myth of trees bearing shells which, on opening, hatch into barnacle geese! This puts the comments about mushrooms in a slightly different light. The fungal illustrations for the improved second edition of 1633 were all taken from Clusius' *Fungorum Historia* of 1601, but do not include a picture of field mushroom (*Agaricus campestris*). There is a plate entitled 'Fungus Virilis Penis effigie', the infamous fungus (see page 115) now called stinkhorn (*Phallus impudicus*). The illustration, copied from Clusius, is reproduced upside down. While this might be a classic example of a printer's cock-up (or down in this case), it also suggests that Gerard was writing about something that he had never seen.

John Parkinson's *The Theatre of Plants*, published in 1640, also used illustrations from Clusius, but at least his version of 'phallus hollandicus' (Dodoens' 1554 work was published in Dutch) was the correct way up. Parkinson makes an early reference to the influence of cultural attitudes on the acceptability of eating mushrooms:

> *And because our country neither produceth much variety of good or bad, to like or mislike, our Nation also not being so addicted to the use of them, as the Italians and other nations are, where they grow more plentifully. I will therefore but runne them over briefly and not insist so much on them as in other things of better respect.*

Culpeper's *Complete Herbal* (originally published under the title *The English Physician*), which first appeared in 1653, makes little mention of fungi, although under the heading 'Mushroom' Culpeper writes:

> *Mushrooms are plants more perfect than many people imagine.*

Precisely 100 years later Carl Linnaeus published *Species Plantarum*, heralding a more systematic approach to the classification and naming of plants, although he was rather less successful in his dealings with fungi. The English poet Edmund Spenser was a contempora of Linnaeus. His writing shows how little the British attitude to fungi had changed over 200 years. Under December in *The Shepherd's Calendar*, written in 1759, we find:

Where I was wont to seeke the honey bee
Working her formall rowmes in Wexen frames
The grislie Todestoole growne there might I see
And loathed Paddocks lording on the same.

Paddock was a name given to the toad. The poem provides another example of the supposed link between mushrooms and toads; two evils together. Early 19th century attitudes were still stuck in the same rut, as can be seen in a small section of Shelley's *The Sensitive Plant*, written in 1820:

And plants, at whose names the verse feel loath,
Filled the place with a monstrous undergrowth,
Prickly, and pulpous, and blistering, and blue,
Livid, and starred with a lurid dew.

And agarics, and fungi, with mildew and mould
Started like mist from the wet ground cold;
Pale, fleshy, as if the decaying dead
With a spirit of growth had been animated!

To Shelley and other English writers, fungi had become not just evil inhabitants of moist murky places but the very symbols of death and decay. Dickens continued this theme in Dombey and Son (1848) with his description of the house in which Florence lived, after the death of her brother:

Mildew and mould began to lurk in closets and fungus trees grew in corners of cellars.

The great American naturalist Henry Thoreau was far more positive in his praise of fungi:

The humblest fungus betrays a life akin to our own.
It is a successful poem in its kind. H. Thoreau, 1854

At about the same time the American poet Emily Dickinson drew on her religious and naturalist backgrounds to depict a mushroom as the ultimate betrayer:

MUSHROOM

The mushroom is the elf of plants.
At evening it is not;
At morning in a truffled hut
It stops upon a spot

As if it tarried always;
And yet its whole career
Is shorter than a snake's delay,
And fleeter than a tare.

'Tis vegetation's juggler,
The germ of alibi;
Doth like a bubble antidate,
And like a bubble hie.

I feel as if the grass were pleased
To have it intermit;
The surreptitious scion
Of summer's circumspect.

Had nature any outcast face
Could she a son condemn,
Had nature an Iscariot,
That mushroom, … it is him. Emily Dickinson

It is more than likely that Emily knew of the common name, Jew's ear, for the jelly fungus *Auricularia auricula-judae* and of the folklore that Judas had hanged himself on an elder tree (the most common host for the fungus).

Lewis Carroll's *Alice's Adventures in Wonderland*, first published in 1865, is an early example where literature depicts the effects of hallucinogenic mushrooms (see page 141).

Alice Meets the Caterpillar

There was a large mushroom growing near her, about the same height as herself; and, when she had looked under it, and on both sides of it, it occurred to her that she might as well look and see what was on the top of it. She stretched herself up on tiptoe, and peeped over the edge of the mushroom, and her eyes immediately met those of a large blue caterpillar, that was sitting on the top with its arms folded, quietly smoking a long hookah, and taking not the smallest notice of her or of anything else.

Sadly, the wonderful illustrations of Tenniel, including one of the hookah-smoking caterpillar sitting on a mushroom, were not in colour. There is little doubt in the minds of many that the caterpillar was sitting on a fly agaric (*Amanita muscaria*).

In a minute or two the Caterpillar took the hookah out of its mouth and yawned once or twice, and shook itself. Then it got down off the mushroom, and crawled away into the grass, merely remarking as it went, 'One side will make you grow taller, and the other side will make you grow shorter.'

After a while she remembered that she still held the pieces of mushroom in her hands, and she set to work very carefully, nibbling first one and then at the other, and growing sometimes taller and sometimes shorter, until she had succeeded in bringing herself down to her usual height.

At this stage of her adventures Alice had already met the White Rabbit and was shortly to find herself at a tea party along with the March Hare, the Hatter and a very sleepy

Dormouse. Of interest to mycologists is where the idea of changes in the perception of size came from. The Reverend Charles Dodgson (Lewis Carroll's real name) started work on his story a few years before its publication. It seems likely that his attention was drawn by a fungus article by Mordecai Cooke in the *Gardener's Chronicle* and he may have seen Cooke's book published in 1862, *A Plain and Easy Account of the British Fungi* (see page 182). The first plate in the book is a colour picture of the red and white fly agaric, alongside an account of its use in Siberia as a means of intoxication and the effects it caused:

> *Erroneous impressions of size and distance are common occurrences: a straw lying in the road becomes a formidable object, to overcome which a leap is taken sufficient to clear a barrel of ale, or the prostrate trunk of a British oak.*

Charles Kingsley may have used the same source for *Hereward, Last of the English*, published in 1866. In the book a Lappish nurse makes use of scarlet toadstools to gain secrets from men she has drugged.

The depiction of the negative side of fungi continued well into the 20th century:

> *The rain had ceased at last, and a sickly autumn sun shone upon a land that was soaked and sodden with water. Wet and rotten leaves reeked and festered under the foul haze which rose from the woods. The fields were spotted with monstrous fungi of a size and colour never matched before – scarlet and mauve and liver and black. It was as though the sick earth had burst forth into foul pustules; mildew and lichen mottled the walls, and with that filthy crop, Death sprang also from the water soaked earth.*
>
> *Arthur Conan Doyle*, Sir Nigel, 1906

D.H. Lawrence, like Emily Dickinson, was a very observant naturalist, as is evident in his poetry and the many nature references in his novels. His 1923 poem *How Beastly the Bourgeois Is* condemns members of the upper class by comparing them to a mushroom:

How beastly the borgeois is
Especially the male of the species –

Nicely groomed, like a mushroom
standing there so sleek and erect and eyeable –
and like a fungus, living on the remains of bygone life,
sucking his own life out of the dead leaves of greater life than his own.

An Excrescence; A Fungus; Alias – A Toadstool upon a Dung-hill (1791) by Hannah Humphrey

And even so, he's stale, he's been here too long.
Touch him, and you'll find he's all gone inside
just like an old mushroom, all wormy inside, and hollow
under a smooth skin and an upright appearance.

Full of seething, wormy, hollow feelings
rather nasty –
How beastly the bourgeois is!

Standing in their thousands, these appearances, in damp England
what a pity they can't all be kicked over
like sickening toadstools, and left to melt back, swiftly
into the soil of England.

This is a poem based on close observation; anyone who has picked an old mushroom full of maggots will appreciate the reference to being hollow under the skin. The plea that they be 'kicked over like sickening toadstools' accurately records the typically British attitude to fungi in the first half of the 20th century.

It is not surprising to find that poisonous fungi have featured regularly as causes of death in murder mystery stories. Storyline inaccuracies are many, usually reflecting the author's lack of scientific knowledge. The queen of the genre, Dorothy L. Sayers, must have thought that she had circumvented this problem when she co-wrote *The Documents in the Case* (1930) with Robert Eustace, the pen name of a physician who wrote medicolegal thrillers. Central to the plot is a man who enjoys eating wild mushrooms. He is found dead after having apparently consumed fly agaric (*Amanita muscaria*) in mistake for the (edible) blusher (*Amanita rubescens*). The cause of death was declared to be muscarine poisoning with the fly agarics as the likely source.

One member of the dead man's family doubts that his uncle would have confused the two species. Further investigation reveals that the muscarine found in the dead man's body was of synthetic origin, as revealed by its ability to rotate a beam of polarised light in an opposite direction to that of naturally occurring muscarine. The lover of the dead man's wife is found to have stolen synthetic muscarine from a local college, before dosing the blushers. So it was murder all along.

In the late 1920s, fly agaric was believed to contain high levels of muscarine, as indicated by its scientific name. It was not until the 1960s that this was found to be false. There is an insignificant amount of the chemical in each fruitbody. More significantly, the chemicals that are present rarely prove fatal. Ironically, although fly agaric is no longer considered to be so dangerous, the reverse is true with the blusher. Good modern books on edible mushrooms point out that it must be well cooked as it contains a chemical that destroys red blood cells; fortunately, this is destroyed by the heat of cooking.

Fungi have been a common thread in science fiction and fantasy novels. A white mushroom nearly 40 feet high features in *Journey to the Centre of the Earth*, Jules Verne's groundbreaking novel first published in 1864. Forty years later H.G. Wells in *Food of the Gods* (1904) has a puffball 'rising like a roc's egg out of the abnormally coarsened turf'. Aldous Huxley became fascinated by the food of the gods in the form of soma, the mythical drug central to his 1932 novel *Brave New World*. While many have argued that soma was of fungal origin (see page 148), others put the case for a plant product (such as cannabis or mescaline). Huxley's last novel *Island* returned to a similar theme, but in this case the moksha drug was used for entertainment and self-knowledge and was described as a yellow mushroom.

In the 30 years between *Brave New World* and *Island*, the American west coast culture was born, fuelled by the discovery of LSD and an increased knowledge of the hallucinogenic effects of peyote (the 'cactus' source of mescaline) and *Psilocybe* mushrooms (see page 141). The effect of this was to burst on to the literary scene in 1962, the same year that *Island* was published. *One Flew over the Cuckoo's Nest* brought fame to author Ken Kesey and later to Jack Nicholson for his film portrayal of the hero, modelled on the author's own experiences with LSD and working in a mental institution.

Tom Wolfe's classic of the counter-culture generation, *The Electric Kool Aid Acid Test*, tells the story of a group ('the merry pranksters'), including Kesey, who travelled across the States in a dayglo-painted school bus and gave new meaning to the word 'trip'. Kesey's infamous acid tests, drug-fuelled parties, included a mushroom concoction known as kool aid. The parties are said to have influenced the poetry of Allen Ginsberg.

By the 1960s the indirect influence of mushrooms on the arts even impinged on popular music. The decade started with 4 weeks at the top of the charts for Lonnie Donegan, singing *My Old Man's a Dustman*, complete with:

I say, I say, I say
(What, you again?)
My dustbin's absolutely full with toadstools
(How do you know it's full?)
'Cos there's not much room inside.

This was a far cry from bands (such as The Grateful Dead) that were to emerge from the American west coast in the 1960s. In 1967 *Surrealistic Pillow* was released by Jefferson Airplane. One track on the album was released as a single a few months later and for over 40 years *White Rabbit* has kept its place as one of the most enigmatic and haunting songs to grace the music scene. Grace was also the name of the composer and singer of the lyrics. She later explained that the words were an answer to all those parents who, having read *Alice's Adventures in Wonderland* to their kids, wondered why the children later experimented with taking drugs.

At the time most radio programmes censored records containing drug references, but *White Rabbit* slipped through, perhaps because the sensors, like so many parents, had not read between the lines of Carroll's 'children's book'. Central to the lyrics are Alice's size-changing experiences after eating mushrooms. Of the haunting last line, Grace Slick used her own artistic licence:

Remember what the Dormouse said: Feed your head ... Feed your head.

This is not a direct quote from the Hatter's tea party; the nearest we get to it is later in the book during the tart-stealing Knave's trial:

'But what did the Dormouse say?' one of the jury asked.
'That I can't remember,' said the Hatter.

Modern classical music also has examples of a fungal influence. Lepo Sumera's *Seenekantaat* (Mushroom Cantata) is a 20 minute work finished in 1983 and performed by a mixed chorus, flute, piano and percussion. The late Estonian composer wrote that he had come into contact with mushrooms and their inner life in 1977. The four movements are spring mushrooms, poisonous ones, autumn mushrooms and the most delicious sorts.

Mushrooms were to play an important role in the success of one of Walt Disney's early films. When *Fantasia* was first released in 1940 it was a commercial failure. The film started as a Mickey Mouse short, based on Goethe's story *The Sorcerer's Apprentice*, set to the music of Paul Dukas. Mickey plays the sorcerer who cannot control some magic that he tries when his boss is out. With images of fly agarics and broomsticks, the magic was obviously of fungal origin. The completed, longer, animated film, based on a collection of popular music pieces was, in many ways, ahead of its time. By the late 1960s *Fantasia* had become a favourite of students and others, many of whom took cannabis or LSD to enhance their enjoyment of the film. The 1969 reissue was even advertised by Disney with a psychedelic-style poster. Finally, the film began to make a profit.

While *Fantasia* was something of a slow burner, the Noddy books, written by Enid Blyton between 1949 and 1963, were instant successes. Adventures in Toyland are still appearing on television nearly 60 years after the characters were first created. Noddy's best friend is a wise bearded gnome who lives in a toadstool house which is obviously modelled on the red and white fly agaric (*Amanita muscaria*). As a child Enid spent many holidays on Brownsea Island in Poole Harbour. The well-wooded island is liberally studded with fly agarics from late summer onwards. The hallucinogenic fly agaric may well lie behind the spell-making gnome, better known as Big Ears.

Attitudes to mushrooms were finally on the change in the more conventional arts world. Sylvia Plath's *Mushrooms* takes a more light-hearted view, in marked contrast to the works of Shelley, Lawrence and Dickinson.

MUSHROOMS

Overnight, very
Whitely, discreetly,
Very quietly
Our toes, our noses
Take hold on the loam,
Acquire the air.
Nobody sees us,
Stops us, betrays us;
The small grains make room.
Soft fists insist on
Heaving the needles,

The leafy bedding,
Even the paving.
Our hammers, our rams,
Earless and eyeless,
Perfectly voiceless,
Widen the crannies,
Shoulder through holes. We
Diet on water,
On crumbs of shadow,
Bland-mannered, asking
Little or nothing.
So many of us!
So many of us!
We are shelves, we are
Tables, we are meek,
We are edible,
Nudgers and shovers
In spite of ourselves.
Our kind multiplies:
We shall by morning
Inherit the earth.
Our foot's in the door.

Sylvia Plath,
The Colossus and Other Poems, 1960

Fungi have even found their way into cartoons. One of the regular Victorian fungal foragers and a contemporary of Mordecai Cooke was Worthington G. Smith. He produced a series of cartoons depicting members of the Woolhope Club on their October forays around Hereford.

Georges Remi, better known as Hergé, introduced the character of Tintin in 1929. Among his many adventures was *The Shooting Star* (1946), where Tintin and his dog Snowy encounter an exploding red and white mushroom on a newly landed Arctic meteorite. More recently Raymond Briggs, created *Fungus the Bogeyman* (1977), a

Morel (*Morchella esculenta*) (1994) by Jessica Tcherepnine

cartoon character who lives with his wife Mildew and son Mould. The antics of Fungus delighted a generation of children and their parents. Cartoons of a very different nature are a major reason for the long-running popularity of *Le Gratin Des Champignons* (1986), a French book about edible mushrooms. The text by Georges Becker is accompanied by Roland Sabatier's brilliant cartoons, the enjoyment of which demands little or no knowledge of the French language.

The final decades of the 20th century saw a resurgence of interest in botanical illustration. Many artists began to depict fungi in artwork aimed at the commercial market rather than as illustrations to accompany scientific texts. Foremost among the fungal artists is Suzanne Lucas.

Fungal art of a different sort is found in the work of the environmental artist Chris Drury. A number of his works (1999–2000) are based on fungal spore prints, as typified by *Poison Pie*, 'Spore print and hand written text in white ink on black card listing all the poisonous fungi and their effects on the body'.

The film world in 2007 was graced by two very different films about mushrooms. Tom Tagholm's 15 minute film *A Bout de Truffle* is a tragicomic tale of a truffle hunter and his pig. The film reached the shortlist of the British Independent Film Awards for the best British short film. In marked contrast, Paddy Breathnach's *Shrooms* was a feature-length horror movie about five American students on a camping 'trip' to Ireland. The trip was provided by some especially Irish magic mushrooms.

One away or another, fungi have certainly left their mark on the arts.

Further Information

British Mycological Society
www.britmycolsoc.org.uk
Information about the society, membership, meetings and publications. Information about *Field Mycology*, a quarterly magazine published by Elsevier. Contat details for local fungus groups.

Fungal societies and local groups
www.fungus.org.uk

Plantlife
www.plantlife.org.uk
A charity that encompasses the conservation of mushrooms and toadstools

Mycological Group, Royal Botanic gardens, Kew
www.rbgkew.org.uk/scihort/mycolexp.html
Information on research and the collection of fungal specimens.

The Royal Botanic gardens, Edinburgh
www.rbge.org.uk/research/celtica/fc.htm
Website with information on Scottish fungi

Northern Ireland Fungus Group
www.nifg.org.uk

Images of Fungi on the Internet
www.fungi.fvlmedia.dkin2.dk

Fungal Records Database of Britain and Ireland
http://194.203.77.76/fieldmycology
Information on the frequency of British fungi

British Wildlife Magazine (bi-monthly)
www.britishwildlife.com
Excellent well illustrated research-led articles including up to date information about fungi

Useful books

Spooner, B. and Roberts, P (2005). *Fungi*. Collins New Naturalist
A mine of up to date information about all things fungal.

Phillips, R. (2006). *Mushrooms*. Macmillan
Covers over 1,200 species with excellent photographs.

Harding, P. (2006) *need to Know? Mushroom Hunting*. Collins
How to safely identify edible wild mushrooms with cooking hints.

Bibliography

Allegro, J.M. (1970). *The Sacred Mushroom and the Cross.* London: Hodder & Stoughton.

Baker, T. (1990). The word 'toadstool' in Britain. *The Mycologist* 4(1): 25–29.

Benjamin, D.R. (1995). *Mushrooms: Poisons and Panaceas. A Handbook for Naturalists, Mycologists, and Physicians.* New York: W. H. Freeman.

Bolton, G. (2000). A Christmas Gift from Siberia. *The British Journal of General Practice.* December.

Breitenbach, J. & Kranzlin, F. (1986). *Fungi of Switzerland. Vol 2: Non gilled fungi.* Lucerne: Verlag Mycologia.

Briggs, R. (1977). *Fungus the Bogeyman.* London: Hamish Hamilton.

Carroll, L. (1865). *Alice's Adventures in Wonderland.*

Cooke, M.C. (1862). *A Plain and Easy Account of the British Fungi.* London: Robert Hardwicke.

Cooke, M.C. (Ed. By Berkeley, M. J. 1875). *Fungi: Their Nature, Influence, and Uses.* London: Henry S. King.

Cooke, M.C. (1891). *British Edible Fungi: How to Distinguish and how to Cook them.* London: Kegan Paul, Trench, Trubner.

Cooke, R.C. (1977). *Fungi, man and his environment.* London: Longman.

Cooke, R.C. (1981). *Fungi.* London: Collins

Conran, S. (1975). *Superwoman.*

Culpepper, N. (1653). *The English Physician or The Complete Herbal.* Foulsham.

Davidson, A. (2002). *The Penguin Companion to Food.* London: Penguin.

Dickens, C. (1848). *Dombey and Son.*

Dickinson, E. (1924). *Complete Poems.* Boston: Little, Brown

Dioscorides (AD 65). *De Materia Medica.*

Doyle, A.C. (1906). *Sir Nigel.*

Drury, C. (2000). *Journeys on Paper.* London: Stephen Lacey Gallery.

English, M.P. (1987). *Mordecai Cubitt Cooke: Victorian Naturalist, Mycologist, Teacher & Eccentric.* Bristol: Biopress.

Evans, S. (2003). Conservation Corner (BAP fungi). *Field Mycology.* 4(1): 32–34.

Findlay, W.P.K. (1967). *Wayside and Woodland Fungi.* London: Frederick Warne

Findlay, W.P.K. (1982). *Fungi, Fiction, & Fact.* Surrey: Richmond Publishing.

Fowles, J. and Horrat, F. (1979). *The Tree.* London: Aurum Press.

Fungus Conservation Forum (2001). *Managing your land with fungi in mind.*

Furst, P.E. (1988). *The Encyclopedia of Psychoactive Drugs. Mushrooms. Psychedelic Fungi.* London: Burke.

Gerard, J. (1597). *The Herball, or Generall Historie of Plantes.* London.

Graves, R. (1981). *The Greek Myths.* London: Penguin.

Greig, B.J.W., Gregory, S. C. & Strouts, R. G. (1991). *Forestry Commission Bulletin* 100. *Honey Fungus.* London: HMSO

Griffith, G., Bratton, J.H. & Easton, G. (2004). Charismatic megafungi: the conservation of waxcap grasslands. *British Wildlife* 16 (1): 31–43.

Grigson, J. (1975). *The Mushroom Feast.* London: Michael Joseph.

Harding, P., Lyon, T. & Tomblin, G. (1996). *How to Identify Edible Mushrooms.* London: HarperCollins.

Harding, P. (1996). *Collins gem Mushrooms.* London: HarperCollins

Harding, P (2007). *the Christmas book.* London: Metro.

Harding, P. (2006). *Need to Know? Mushroom Hunting.* London: Collins.

Heim, R. (1978). *Les Champignons Toxiques et Hallucinogenes.* 2nd *Ed.* Paris: Boubee

Hergé (1946, 2002 Ed). *The Adventures of Tintin. The Shooting Star.* Egmont Books.

Holden, L. (Ed) (2003). *List of Recommended English Names for Fungi.* Penrith: Summerfield Books.

Holden, L. and Hamper, K. (2003). *The Fungi Name Trail.* F.S.C. Publications.

Hooker, J.D. (1854). *Himalayan Journals.*

Hudler, G. W. (1998). *Magical Mushrooms, Mischievous Molds.* Princeton University Press.
Huxley, A. (1932). *Brave New World.* Chatto & Windus
Huxley, A. (1962). *Island.* Chatto & Windus
Jay, E., Noble, M. and Hobbs, A. S. (1992). *A Victorian Naturalist. Beatrix Potter's Drawings from the Armitt Collection.* Frederik Warne
Kesey, K. (1962). *One Flew over the Cuckoo's Nest.*
Kingsley, C. (1866). *Hereward, Last of the English.*
Lange, M. & Hora, F. B. (1963). *Collins Guide to Mushrooms & Toadstools.* London: Collins
Large, E. C. (1940). *The Advance of The Fungi.* London: Jonathan Cape.
Lawrence, D. H. (1923). *How Beastly the Bourgeois Is.*
Legon, N.W. & Henrici, A. (2005). *Checklist of the British & Irish Basidiomycota.* Richmond: Royal Botanic Gardens, Kew.
Linnaeus, C. (1753). *Species Plantarum.*
Mabey, R. (1972). *Food for Free.* London: Collins.
Marren, P. (2006). Derek Reid – obituary. *The Independent.* January 28th
Marren, P. (2006). The 'global fungal weeds': the toadstools of wood-chip beds. *British Wildlife.* 18(2): 98–105.
Marren, P. (2007). Wildlife reports – fungi (Red Data list). *British Wildlife.* 18(3): 217
Matossian, M. K. (1989). *Poisons of the Past: Molds, Epidemics and History.* New Haven: Yale University Press.
Mattock, G. (2002). Fungi upon other fungi grow: Britain's parasitic toadstools. *British Wildlife.* 14 (2) 117–122.
Merryweather, J. (2001). Meet the Glomales – the ecology of mycorrhiza. *British Wildlife.* 13(2): 86–93.
Ministry of Agriculture & Fisheries. (1945 6th Ed.). *Edible and Poisonous Fungi.* London: His Majesty's Stationery Office.
Morgan, A. (1995). *Toads and Toadstools.* Berkeley: Celestial Arts.
Nichols, J. B. (1932). *Down the Garden Path.* J Cape
Parkinson, J. (1640). *The Theatre of Plants.*
Philips, R. (2006). *Mushrooms.* London: Macmillan.
Plath, S. (1960). *Mushroom* from *The Colossus and Other Poems.* London: Harper and Row.
Pliny, C. (AD 77). *Historia Naturalis.*
Potter (1988). *Potter's New Cyclopedia of British Drugs and Preparations.*
Ramsbottom, J. (1953). *Mushrooms and Toadstools.* New Naturalist 7. London: Collins.
Reid, D. A. (1980). *Mushrooms & Toadstools.* Ward Lock
Rice, M. & Beebee, D. (1980). *Mushrooms For Color.* California: Mad River Press.
Rocchia, J. (1995). *Truffles: the black diamond and other kinds.* Avignon: Editions A. Barthelemy.
Roberts, P. & Spooner, B. (2000). Sending fungi to Kew. *Field Mycology* 1(1): 4–5.
Rudgley, R. (1993). *The Alchemy of Culture. Intoxicants in Society.* London: British Museum Press.
Sayers, D. L. & Eustace, R. (1930). *The Documents in the Case.* London: Victor Gollancz.
Sheehan, J. C. & Wainwright, M. (1990). *Miracle Cure: The Story of Penicillin and the Golden Age of Antibiotics.* Oxford: Blackwell.
Shelley, P. B. (1820). *The Sensitive Plant.*
Smith, M. L., Bruhn, J. N. and Anderson, J. A. (1992). The fungus *Armillaria bulbosa* is among the largest and oldest of living organisms. *Nature.* 356: 428–431.
Spenser, E. (1759). *The Shepherd's Calendar.*
Spooner, B. & Roberts, P. (2005). *Fungi.* New Naturalist 96. London: Collins.
Step, E. (1913). *Toadstools and Mushrooms of the countryside.* London: Hutchinson.
Sumera, L. (2005). *Mushroom Cantata & other choral works.* BIS Records
Taylor, R. (1980). Who is Santa Claus? *Sunday Times.* Dec 21st.
Thoreau, H. (1854) Walden.
Trostanestesky, A. (2005). Home cultivation of edible woodland mushrooms. *Field Mycology.* 6(1): 5–7.
Twain, M. (1884). *The Adventures of Huckleberry Finn.*
Verne, J. (1864). *Journey to the Centre of the Earth.*
Wakefield, E. M. (1958). *The Observer's Book of Common Fungi.* London: Frederick Warne.
Wasson, R. G. (1957). Seeking the magic Mushroom. *Life* 49 (19): 100–120.
Wasson, R. G. (1968). *Soma: Divine Mushroom of Immortality.* New York: Harcourt Brace Jovanovich.
Wasson, R. G. & V. P. (1957). *Mushrooms, Russia & History.* New York: Pantheon.
Watling, R. (2003). *Fungi.* London: The Natural History Museum.
Wells, H. G. (1904). *Food of the Gods.*
Wolfe, T. (1968). *The Electric Kool Aid Acid Test.*

Index

Page numbers in *italics* indicate illustrations or photographs.

PICTURE CREDITS

2 Lauros/Giraudon/The Bridgeman Art Library (BAL); 6 Archives Charmet/BAL; 10 Giraudon/BAL; 14 SPL; 18 Laurie Campbell/NHPA; 22 Archives Charmet/BAL; 24 M I Walker/NHPA; 26 Stephen Dalton/NHPA; 28 Yves Lanceau/NHPA; Simon Booth/NHPA; 35 Brian Hawkes/NHPA; 36 Laurie Campbell/NHPA; 39 Brian Hawkes/NHPA; 40 Laurie Campbell/NHPA; 42 John & Sue Buckingham/NHPA; 44 Joe Blossom/NHPA; 45, 48 Laurie Campbell/NHPA; 50 Jeremy Burgess/NHPA; 55 Martin Garwood/NHPA; 58 Yves Lanceau/NHPA; 60 George Bernard/NHPA; 62 Simon Booth/NHPA; 65 Martin Garwood/NHPA; 69 Yves Lanceau/NHPA; 71 Guy Edwardes/NHPA; 72 Laurie Campbell/NHPA; 74 George Bernard/NHPA; 77 UPPA/Photoshot; 78 Vaughan Fleming/SPL; 80 Stephen Dalton/NHPA; 84 Lutra/NHPA; 86 Alinari/BAL; 88 Tse Ka Yin/Photoshot; 91 Photoshot; 94 Bob Gibbons/SPL; 98 Ivan Polunin /NHPA; 100 Simon Booth/NHPA; 102 Brian Hawkes/NHPA; 108 Simon Booth/NHPA; 113 Stephen Dalton/NHPA; 114 Mike Lane/NHPA; 116 Guy Edwardes/NHPA; 119 Laurie Campbell/NHPA; 122 Helmut Moik/NHPA; 126 Simon Booth/NHPA; 128 M I Walker/NHPA; 130, 133 Yves Lanceau/NHPA; 136 Archives Charmet/The Bridgeman Art Library; 139 John Walsh/SPL; 142 National Library, St. Petersburg, Russia/BAL; 148 Mike Lane/NHPA; 154 The Stapleton Collection/BAL; 158 Laurie Campbell/NHPA; 164 David Scharf/SPL; 168 Gustoimages/SPL; 170 Jean-Lour Charmet/SPL; 179 Image-Quest 3D/NHPA; 186 Beatrix Potter/Frank Warne; 190 Natural History Museum, London/BAL; 194 John Tenniel/BAL; 196 James Gillray/BAL; 202 BAL